Using RTI

to Teach Literacy *to* Diverse Learners, K–8

Using RTI
to Teach Literacy *to* Diverse Learners, K–8
STRATEGIES FOR THE INCLUSIVE CLASSROOM

SHEILA ALBER-MORGAN

CORWIN

A SAGE Company

For information:

Corwin
A SAGE Company
2455 Teller Road
Thousand Oaks, California 91320
(800) 233-9936
Fax: (800) 417-2466
www.corwin.com

SAGE Ltd.
1 Oliver's Yard
55 City Road
London EC1Y 1SP
United Kingdom

SAGE India Pvt. Ltd.
B 1/I 1 Mohan Cooperative
    Industrial Area
Mathura Road, New Delhi 110 044
India

SAGE Asia-Pacific Pte. Ltd.
33 Pekin Street #02-01
Far East Square
Singapore 048763

Printed in the United States of America

Library of Congress Cataloging-in-Publication Data

Alber, Sheila Rene, 1963-
Using RTI to teach literacy to diverse learners, K–8: strategies for the inclusive classroom/Sheila Alber-Morgan.
    p. cm.
Includes bibliographical references and index.
ISBN 978-1-4129-6952-9 (pbk.)

  1. Language arts. 2. Language arts—Remedial teaching. 3. Inclusive education.
4. School failure—Prevention. I. Title.

LB1576.A61 2010
372.6—dc22   2010001677

This book is printed on acid-free paper.

10 11 12 13 14 10 9 8 7 6 5 4 3 2 1

Acquisitions Editor:	Jessica Allan
Associate Editor:	Sarah Bartlett
Production Editor:	Amy Schroller
Copy Editor:	Nancy Conger
Typesetter:	C&M Digitals (P) Ltd.
Proofreader:	Charlotte J. Waisner
Indexer:	Jean Casalegno
Cover Designer:	Karine Hovsepian

Contents

Acknowledgments

Corwin gratefully acknowledges the contributions of the following individuals:

Emma Barnes, K–2 Literacy Facilitator
Hawk Ridge Elementary School
Charlotte, NC

John Celletti, Adjunct Professor and Behavior Specialist
University of Detroit Mercy and Lincoln Park School District
Detroit, MI

Jeanne Danneker, Professor of Special Education
Winona State University
Winona, MN

Stacey Ferguson, First-, Second-, and Third-Grade Teacher
North Bay Elementary School
Bay Saint Louis, MS

Mari Gates, Special Education Teacher/Fifth-Grade General Education
    Inclusion Teacher
Henry B. Burkland Intermediate School
Middleboro, MA

Cathy Hooper, Literacy Coordinator
Henderson Independent School District
Henderson, TX

Sharon Judge, Associate Dean
Graduate Studies and Assessment
University Norfolk
Norfolk, VA

Shelly Kelly, Literacy Teacher
Chief Joseph Elementary
Great Falls Public Schools
Great Falls, MT

About the Author

 **Sheila Alber-Morgan** has been an associate professor of special education at The Ohio State University since 2005. She was also a faculty member at The University of Southern Mississippi for eight years. After teaching for several years in inclusive classrooms in both urban and rural South Carolina, Dr. Alber-Morgan began doctoral training at The Ohio State University and earned her PhD in 1997. For the past 15 years, Dr. Alber-Morgan's research has focused on examining the effects of various literacy interventions on the learning outcomes of elementary and secondary students with and without disabilities. Additionally, her research incorporates strategies for programming for generalization and maintenance of academic and social skills. Almost all of Dr. Alber-Morgan's research has been designed and implemented in collaboration with classroom teachers, and she has over 50 research and practitioner publications including peer-reviewed journal articles, textbook ancillaries, and book chapters.

For David

community rather than just visitors. The three dimensions of inclusive practices described by Friend and Bursuck (2009) are physical, social, and instructional integration. Physical integration is placement with nondisabled peers in a general education classroom. Social integration is fostering relationships with peers, and instructional integration is teaching students the same curriculum while providing any necessary accommodations to ensure success. The Response to Intervention (RTI) model has become a popular and effective way to provide differentiated instruction in inclusive classrooms (Gersten et al., 2009). Additionally, special education law (IDEIA, 2004) encourages the use of RTI as a way to prevent reading problems and identify students with learning disabilities.

RTI AND ASSESSMENT

The Individuals with Disabilities Education Improvement Act (IDEIA, 2004) allows states to identify students with learning disabilities based on how well they respond to evidence-based teaching methods (that is, their responsiveness to intervention). The RTI model also provides an evidence-based way to manage instruction for all students in inclusive classrooms using a multitiered approach (Gersten et al., 2009). Based on experimental research, a panel of experts from the National Center for Educational Evaluation (Gersten et al.) made the following general recommendations for implementing multitiered interventions:

- Tier 1: Screen every student at the beginning and middle of the school year and frequently monitor the progress of struggling learners. Based on assessment of student needs, provide differentiated instruction for students at their individual reading levels.
- Tier 2: For students not responding successfully to Tier 1 instruction, provide more intensive intervention three to five times per week (for 20 to 40 minutes) to students in small groups. Monitor progress and determine if Tier 3 intervention is necessary.
- Tier 3: Provide daily intensive instruction on targeted literacy skills with opportunities for one-on-one instruction, frequent practice, and systematic feedback. Tier 3 interventions should be planned with input from the school's intervention assistance team.

The RTI model is ideal for serving the needs of diverse learners because interventions and materials can be customized to the backgrounds, abilities, and experiences of individual learners (Brown-Chidsey & Steege, 2005). In order to implement RTI effectively, teachers need an accurate and reliable assessment system for monitoring progress to determine which students are responding to intervention and which students need more intensive supplemental instruction (Vaughn et al., 2008). Effective progress monitoring provides teachers with a reliable prediction of student achievement (Deno, 2003) and enables teachers to increase student achievement by making more effective instructional decisions (Fuchs & Fuchs, 2006). Curriculum-based measurement (CBM) is an evidence-based progress monitoring system that works well in the context of the RTI model.

Curriculum-Based Measurement

In 1985, an article by Stan Deno, "Curriculum-Based Measurement: The Emerging Alternative," was published in *Exceptional Children.* This article was identified as one of the 10 most influential publications in special education literature since 1960 (McLesky, 2004). Derived from the principles of applied behavior analysis, Deno introduced CBM as a method of data collection, with standardized procedures enabling teachers to continuously monitor student progress of academic skills. In addition to assessing a student's level of performance, repeated CBM measures over time can also provide an accurate picture of each student's rate of learning (Deno, 2003). With CBM, the teacher frequently administers brief and direct timed probes of basic skills. For example, to assess reading fluency, the teacher times a student for one minute as he reads a passage, then counts and records the number of words the student reads correctly and incorrectly.

Several CBM programs are available to teachers (AIMSweb, DIBELS, Edcheckup, for instance). For example, the AIMSweb Progress Monitoring and Response to Intervention System provides teachers with curriculum-based measurement materials for assessing reading, writing, mathematics, spelling, early literacy, and early numeracy. CBM probes are easy and quick to administer and score, sensitive to small changes in performance, and can predict student performance over time (Cusumono, 2007). Using the results of CBM probes, teachers chart student performance and examine the data to determine if students are progressing at the expected rate. In addition to helping teachers make timely instructional decisions, CBM can help teachers make better use of instructional time. That is, they can spend less time testing and more time teaching (Hosp, Hosp, & Howell, 2007).

Special education teachers first used CBM, but the number of general education classroom teachers using CBM has been increasing. Because CBM is efficient and technically adequate, it fits in well with the RTI model (Hosp et al., 2007). In an RTI model, the same CBMs can be used across all three tiers. Only the frequency of assessment varies across students depending on their needs (Hosp et al.). In this book, Chapter 2 (Assessing for Intervention in Reading) and Chapter 4 (Assessing for Intervention in Writing) focus on procedures for using CBM to assess and monitor reading and writing performance in inclusive classrooms. In addition to CBM, Chapters 2 and 4 will provide teachers with suggestions for using authentic assessments as a way to supplement CBM and provide more comprehensive information about student abilities. Authentic assessment refers to evaluating meaningful products that require a synthesis of skills (for example, written stories or reports, oral presentations).

Using CBM and additional assessment information to guide instructional decision making, teachers may plan and implement evidence-based practices for each level of intensity in the RTI model. Researchers have identified evidence-based reading and writing practices and programs within each tier of the RTI model. Chapter 3 (Implementing Multitiered Reading Instruction) and Chapter 5 (Implementing Multitiered Writing Instruction) focus on evidence-based practices for teaching language arts using a multitiered approach and managing differentiated literacy instruction.

RTI AND LITERACY INSTRUCTION

Most people think of literacy as the ability to read and write. In addition to reading and writing, the Workforce Investment Act of 1998 includes in its definition speaking, computing, and problem solving in the context of developing potential and achieving goals. The United Nations Educational, Scientific, and Cultural Organization (UNESCO, 2004) states that literacy is "the ability to identify, understand, interpret, create, communicate, compute and use printed and written materials associated with varying contexts" (p. 13). Furthermore, UNESCO defines literacy as a continuum of learning that allows individuals to develop their knowledge, achieve their goals, and participate fully in their communities. McKenna, Labbo, Reinking, & Zucker (2007) describe an evolving idea of literacy that extends to computer technology skills. Because digital technology is so pervasive in all aspects of current society, embedding technology into literacy instruction may be critical for preparing students to be literate adults in a high-tech society. Additionally, many reading and writing computer programs have been demonstrated to be effective for increasing a range of reading and writing skills (MacArthur, 2009).

This book presents evidence-based programs and practices that incorporate reading, writing, speaking, listening, and computer literacy. Specifically, Chapter 3 and Chapter 5 will provide teachers with specific learning activities for each level of a three-tiered RTI model. In general, literacy research has demonstrated that all students, especially those with diverse needs, benefit a great deal from explicit teaching, active student responding, peer-mediated learning, programming for generalization, integrating the language arts, and collaborative teaching. This book will address how each of these practices can be used to teach literacy in inclusive classrooms within the RTI model.

Explicit Instruction and Active Student Responding

Explicit instruction is directly teaching a skill using modeling, guided practice, and systematic feedback. Teachers can provide explicit instruction using a model-lead-test sequence (Engelmann & Carnine, 1982). First, the teacher models the skill (for example, "This word is *tomorrow.*"); then the teacher and students perform the skill together ("Let's read this word together, *tomorrow.*"); finally, the students perform the skill alone (with the teacher telling them, "Now you read the word."). For each student response, the teacher provides immediate feedback. If the students make an error, the teacher uses a consistent systematic error correction procedure (such as telling the students the correct answer, having the students repeat the answer, and presenting the learning trial again).

In order to be proficient with any skill, students need frequent opportunities to actively respond to instruction (that is, they learn by doing; Heward, 1994). Students are engaging in active student responding (ASR) when they make an observable response to instruction (such as speaking, writing). In reading, for example, students are making active responses when they pronounce letter sounds, read sight words aloud, or write the answers to comprehension questions.

ASR techniques will be most effective for increasing achievement if they provide for frequent response opportunities, a clear response prompt (Teacher says, "What word?"), and immediate feedback for each response ("Correct, the word is *car*."). In addition to being effective for all students, ASR techniques are ideal for the inclusive classroom because all children can participate simultaneously as part of one unified group. Evidence-based ASR activities presented in this book include choral responding, response cards, and guided notes.

Peer-Mediated Instruction

Another way to promote active student responding is through peer-mediated instruction such as class-wide peer tutoring or cooperative learning groups. In peer-mediated arrangements, students work together in pairs or groups to practice academic skills and provide each other with immediate feedback. Ideal for inclusive classrooms, peer-mediated programs are highly structured teaching arrangements that can supplement and strengthen the effectiveness of balanced literacy programs. Peer-mediated instruction provides students with frequent opportunities to make academic responses and receive immediate feedback. When peer-mediated instruction is implemented correctly, *all* students benefit. Decades of research demonstrate the effectiveness of peer-mediated instruction for increasing academic achievement and social competence across a wide range of high- and low-performing learners in K–12 classrooms (see Maheady, Harper, & Malette, 2001; McMaster, Fuchs, & Fuchs, 2006). Students who tend to make the greatest gains as a result of peer-mediated instruction include students with disabilities (Allison & Rhem, 2007) and English language learners (Gersten et al., 2007). In addition to promoting cross-cultural friendships, heterogeneous cooperative learning increases the language and literacy skills of diverse learners (Crandall, Jaramillo, Olsen, & Peyton, 2001; Snowman & Biehler, 2003). Chapters 3, 5, 6, and 7 present evidence-based peer-mediated instructional activities for increasing literacy skills in inclusive classrooms.

Integrating Language Arts

Research demonstrates the effectiveness of integrating language arts instruction for increasing student achievement (for example, Shanahan, 2009). Connecting instruction in reading, writing, speaking, and listening is an efficient and authentic way to improve literacy achievement. For example, Abbott and Berninger (1993) found that handwriting skills, letter naming, and spelling skills were related to early decoding proficiency. Foorman and colleagues (2006) found that written expression also had a positive effect on early decoding skills. Additionally, recent research identifies a strong connection between written expression and reading comprehension (Graham & Perin, 2007). In their report of best practices for writing instruction, Graham and Perin identified sentence combining and written text summarization as evidence-based procedures for improving both reading comprehension and written expression. Chapter 6 will provide teachers with direction for planning connected language arts instruction in authentic contexts using thematic units.

Programming for Generalization

For instruction to be truly effective, it must produce generalized outcomes for students. This means that when a student learns a new skill in the classroom, he or she should be able to use that skill independently in a variety of functional ways, in a variety of relevant settings and situations, and over time. Many teachers do not deliberately program for generalization. Instead, they *hope* their students will be able to generalize and maintain new skills. Stokes and Baer (1977) called this approach "train and hope." The problem with this most widely used approach is that it does not work.

When planning instruction for all learners, especially those who struggle, it is imperative that teachers deliberately program instruction that promotes generalization and maintenance of newly learned skills. Fortunately, applied research provides teachers with many effective generalization strategies to incorporate into literacy instruction. Stokes and Baer (1977) and Cooper, Heron, and Heward (2007) describe a variety of strategies designed to promote the transfer of skills from the teaching setting (the classroom) to any number of generalization settings or situations (such as other classrooms, home, community settings). Examples of generalization strategies delineated by Cooper and colleagues (2007) include teaching students the range of representative examples of a concept or skill, incorporating important features of the generalization setting into the training setting, and arranging for students to contact reinforcement in the generalization setting. Chapter 7 describes how teachers can use these kinds of strategies to increase generalization and maintenance of literacy skills.

COLLABORATIVE TEACHING

Collaboration is essential for creating an effective inclusive classroom in which all children are actively engaged in appropriately differentiated and individualized instruction. Three inclusive classroom models requiring collaboration include the consultant model, the teaming model, and the coteaching model. In the consultant model, the general education teacher provides most of the classroom instruction with additional input and guidance from a special education teacher. With teaming, the special education teacher works with a grade-level team (for example, all of the fourth-grade teachers) to help plan appropriate instruction and necessary accommodations for struggling students. In a coteaching model, both general and special education teachers work together to plan and deliver instruction to every student. Both teachers are equally responsible for all student outcomes. Using a coteaching model, the following are examples of different kinds of arrangements for instructional delivery in inclusive classrooms (Vaughn, Bos, & Schumm, 2006).

- *Station teaching.* Two teachers each provide simultaneous instruction to half of the students in the classroom, then the groups switch. Additional independent stations or learning centers can be included in station teaching.
- *Parallel teaching.* The students are separated into two heterogeneous groups and each teacher works with the same group of students for the duration of the lesson.

- *Alternative teaching.* One teacher works with most of the students while another teacher works with a small homogeneous group of students for remediation or enrichment.
- *Teaming.* Both teachers work together to deliver the same content to the whole class (that is, one teacher demonstrates while the other explains, both teachers role-play to demonstrate a skill).

Instructional arrangements should be flexible and frequently varied throughout the day. Using the RTI model, teachers can make collaborative decisions about the most appropriate arrangements that meet student needs and match curricular demands. The likelihood of successful collaboration increases when teachers have effective communication skills, shared responsibility for common goals, time to plan, and administrative support. When teachers collaborate they have the advantage of combining their unique strengths and ideas to create an enriching and vibrant learning environment for every child in the classroom.

SUMMARY

Each child comes to school equipped with his or her own unique set of characteristics, abilities, challenges, dispositions, talents, and needs. Teachers are responsible for designing and implementing instruction that enables individual learners to achieve academic and social competence in and out of the classroom and over time. Using universal design of learning (UDL) as a guiding framework, teachers can incorporate necessary supports into instructional planning so that all students are actively engaged, challenged, and successful. The Response to Intervention (RTI) model is an evidence-based approach to achieving universal design in inclusive classrooms. The RTI model consists of multiple tiers or levels of instruction that become increasingly more intensified for individual students based on their needs as determined by objective assessments. Teachers can use curriculum-based measurement (CBM) to monitor student progress and make instructional decisions about the extent to which students need more intensive support or supplemental instruction. When applied to literacy instruction, teachers can customize the following general teaching procedures within multitiered instruction: explicit teaching, active student responding (choral response, response cards, guided notes), peer-mediated teaching, integrating language arts (listening, speaking, reading, and writing), and programming for generalization. Additionally, collaborative teaching is likely to increase successful literacy instruction for diverse learners in inclusive classrooms.

2

Assessing for Intervention in Reading

RTI AND CBM READING

In Response to Intervention (RTI) models, results of frequent and direct assessments must guide decision making about the type and intensity of multitiered reading instruction. The most useful assessments are sensitive enough to changes in performance to determine whether or not students are responding successfully to intervention. Considering the number of students in inclusive classrooms and their wide range of reading abilities, teachers need a quick, accurate, and reliable system for assessing performance and monitoring progress. Timely assessment information allows teachers to make immediate adjustments to instruction that will increase the likelihood of student achievement. Four purposes of assessment include screening, monitoring progress, making diagnostic decisions, and determining student outcomes

Screening assessments are administered to the whole class to help teachers determine how well the students perform compared to their peers and to identify the students who may need more support or enrichment. Progress-monitoring assessments are administered frequently to provide ongoing information about the extent to which students are responding to intervention. When students are not responding well, they can be given diagnostic assessments to pinpoint specific areas of weakness. Those areas of weakness can then be specifically targeted for intervention. Finally, outcome assessments, required by federal and state law, are administered at the end of the school year to determine the overall effectiveness of the reading program. Curriculum-based measurement (CBM) can be used to accomplish each of the above purposes of assessment. Teachers can objectively examine CBM data to determine the level of intensity needed for each student's success.

Hosp, Hosp, and Howell (2007) recommend administering CBM for student screening and benchmarking at least three times per school year, once per quarter. To avoid over-identifying students at risk, the first screening should be at least two weeks after the school year begins to allow for review and practice of basic skills (Hosp et al.). Students who perform on grade level with the CBM screening assessment will probably respond well to Tier 1 instruction (that is, evidence-based whole-class instruction). Students who score in the bottom 25 percent should be considered at risk for reading failure and will likely need more intensive instruction (Tier 2 small-group instruction or Tier 3 one-on-one instruction).

As teachers implement their literacy programs using multitiered interventions, they can use progress monitoring to determine which students are responding well and which students need more support. The frequency with which teachers collect progress-monitoring data will vary across students based on individual levels of performance. CBM probes for progress monitoring should be administered monthly for higher-performing students and at least weekly for struggling students. Teachers can examine individual progress-monitoring data to determine if instruction is effective or if it needs to be modified. For students who are not responding well to instruction, CBM probes can be supplemented with additional diagnostic assessment information. This will help teachers identify reading problems more specifically and assist with planning Tiers 2 and 3 interventions. At the end of the school year, teachers can use CBM to assess overall reading growth.

CBM READING METHODS

CBM reading is a valid and reliable measure of global reading proficiency, sensitive to small changes in performance and predictive of success on state-mandated assessments (see Good, Simmons, & Kame'enui, 2001; McGlinchey & Hixson, 2004). Useful CBM measures for elementary and secondary reading are oral reading fluency (ORF) and Maze-passage reading. CBM ORF requires the student to read a passage for one minute to assess accuracy and speed. According to Fuchs and Fuchs (2004), ORF CBMs should be used for children in first or second grade and above.

Maze is a CBM in which every seventh word is deleted from a reading passage and replaced with three word choices. As the student silently reads the passage, he selects each correct word choice while being timed for three minutes. Although commercial materials are available for students in grades one through four, Maze is actually most appropriate for assessing students in fourth grade or higher because of its predictive validity of reading proficiency for this population (Fuchs & Fuchs, 2004). CBM ORF and Maze are also good predictors of reading achievement for English language learners (Wiley & Deno, 2005). Additionally, Ramirez and Shapiro (2007) found that bilingual students' oral reading fluency of Spanish text predicted end-of-the-year reading achievement in English.

CBM measures for early reading proficiency may include letter sound fluency (LSF), letter naming fluency (LNF), phoneme segmentation fluency (PSF), word identification fluency (WIF), and nonsense word fluency (NWF). Students are timed for one minute as they read or say a series of letter sounds or words. Early CBM reading enables teachers to prevent future reading problems by identifying students quickly for immediate intervention.

In order to conduct CBM reading, teachers must obtain appropriate assessment materials, administer and score the CBM, graph the CBM data, and make instructional decisions. The following sections are procedures for administering CBM probes for oral reading fluency, Maze, and early reading.

Oral Reading Fluency

Obtaining assessment materials. In order to assess reading fluency, appropriately leveled reading passages are necessary. Reading passages selected for each student's CBM should be equivalent in grade level and contain at least 200 words (that is, more words than the student can orally read in one minute). AIMSweb, Dynamic Indicators of Basic Early Literacy Skills (DIBELS), Edcheckup, and Intervention Central are resources for obtaining leveled reading passages for oral reading fluency.

In order to conduct CBM ORF, the teacher will need one copy of the reading passage for the student to read and one copy to score. The teacher and student copies of the reading passage are the same, except that the teacher's copy will show word totals at the end of each line for scoring ease. The teacher's copy should be attached to a clipboard during testing so the student cannot see it. Other materials include the directions for administration and scoring, a stop watch, and a pencil. Prior to administering CBM, the teacher should become familiar with the administering and scoring directions. See Table 2.1 for CBM resources.

Table 2.1 Curriculum-Based Measurement (CBM) Resources

AIMSweb http://www.aimsweb.com/ Pay Site	Oral Reading Fluency (ORF): Grades 1–8 (available in Spanish) Maze: Grades 1–8 Early Reading (available in Spanish) • Letter Naming Fluency (LNF) • Letter Sound Fluency (LSF) • Phoneme Segmentation Fluency (PSF) • Nonsense Word Fluency (NWF)
DIBELS https://dibels.uoregon.edu/ Pay Site	Oral Reading Fluency (ORF): Grades 1–6 (available in Spanish) Early Reading • Initial Sound Fluency (ISF) • Phoneme Segmentation Fluency (PSF) • Nonsense Word Fluency (NWF)
Edcheckup http://www.edcheckup.com/ Pay Site	Oral Reading Fluency (ORF): Grades 1–6 Maze: Grades 1–6 Early Reading • Letter Sound Fluency (LSF) • Word Identification Fluency (WIF)
Intervention Central http://www.interventioncentral.org/	Oral Reading Fluency: Grades 1–6 Early Reading: (available in Spanish) • Letter Naming Fluency (LNF) • Word Identification Fluency (WIF)

Administering and scoring the CBM ORF. CBM ORF assessments are administered to students individually. Because CBM is standardized, teachers must be sure to follow the directions for administration. The ORF measure should be conducted in a quiet area relatively free of distractions. The teacher places a copy of the reading passage on the desk in front of the student while the teacher has her copy on a clipboard. The teacher should read to the student the scripted directions that are available with the CBM passages.

For example, the AIMSweb manual provides the following script for ORF administration: "When I say 'Begin,' start reading aloud at the top of this page . . . Try to read each word. If you come to a word you don't know, I'll tell it to you. Be sure to do your best reading. Are there any questions?" (Shinn & Shinn, 2002, p. 12). As the student reads, the teacher follows along and marks a slash through any errors. An error is marked each time the student substitutes or mispronounces a word, omits a word, reverses two words (both words are scored as errors), or hesitates for more than three seconds. Teachers should be sure to consider local and individual student dialects when determining whether or not a word is pronounced correctly. An error is not marked if a student inserts a word, repeats a word, or self-corrects a word within three seconds. While the student is engaged in the one-minute timed reading, the teacher should not correct any reading errors. The teacher should only provide the correct word if the student hesitates for more than three seconds. At the end of one minute, the teacher places an end bracket to mark the last word read, and asks the student to stop reading.

After administering the CBM ORF, the teacher calculates the number of words correct per minute (WCPM) by counting the total number of words attempted in one minute and subtracting the number of errors. This score will be plotted on the student's ORF graph. If the student reads fewer than 10 words per minute, the teacher should do another ORF assessment with reading passages from a lower grade level.

Graphing ORF scores. Creating graphs is a good way to organize student data for easy viewing and interpretation. Graphs provide teachers with visual displays of ongoing student performance so that they can more accurately monitor progress. Additionally, graphing student data provides a clear and useful way to communicate with students and their parents about their performance.

In order to graph CBM data, the teacher will need to use graphing paper or a computer program (such as Excel) to create a line graph that shows the level of student progress over time. *Intervention Central* provides preformatted Excel spread sheets to monitor progress. AIMSweb, DIBELS, Edcheckup, and Intervention Central (see Table 2.1) also include tools for monitoring progress and graphing student data.

Begin making the graph by creating a vertical axis and a horizontal axis (see Figure 2.1). The vertical axis will show the value of the student's CBM scores (words correct per minute) and the horizontal axis will show when the student attained those scores (Week 1, Week 2). The horizontal axis should show each week until the end of the school year. Examining the data path will help teachers determine the effectiveness of an intervention and whether or not they need to modify instruction. Figure 2.1

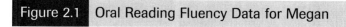

Figure 2.1   Oral Reading Fluency Data for Megan

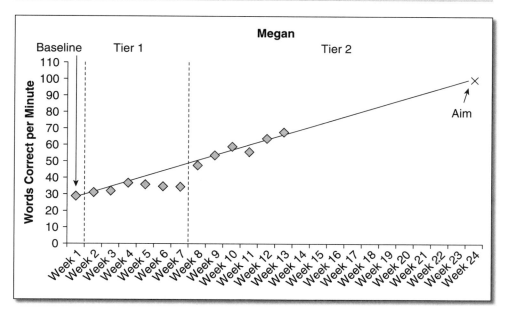

shows an example of a line graph used for monitoring the ORF progress of a second grader with learning disabilities (Megan). Teachers may use the following steps for monitoring student progress using a line graph.

1. *Collect and graph baseline data.* When assessing ORF on the first session, administer three different timed-reading passages of equal difficulty. Then use the median score (that is, the score that numerically falls in between the highest and lowest score) as the first data point on the graph. For example, Megan's scores are 27 WCPM on the first reading, 31 WCPM on the second reading, and 29 WCPM on the third reading, so the median score is 29. The teacher will plot 29 on the graph for the first session.

2. *Set appropriate goals.* Megan's baseline ORF score is 29. In order to set appropriate goals, her teacher should look at the norm table for Reading ORF CBM (available on AIMSweb). The norm tables provided on AIMSweb show norms and percentiles for K–12 students for fall, winter, and spring. For Megan, the norm table shows that a second grader scoring 29 WCPM at the beginning of the school year (in the fall) is reading in the twenty-fifth percentile. To set an appropriately ambitious goal, the teacher should look at the spring column of the norm table to find out how well the students at the fiftieth percentile perform by the end of the school year (in the spring). The norm table on AIMSweb shows that a second grader who scores 100 WCPM in the spring is performing at the fiftieth percentile. If Megan increases her reading rate to 100 WCPM by spring, she will be performing in the average range compared to other second graders. So, Megan's teacher decides that 100 WCPM is an appropriate goal for Megan. Ambitious goals for growth rates

are about one to three words per week for first through fourth graders, and about one word per week for fifth and sixth graders (Fuchs et al., 1993).

3. *Draw an aim line.* The aim line is the line that connects the baseline data point to the goal. Before any intervention data are collected, Megan's teacher draws a line from the first data point (29 WCPM) to her goal (100 WCPM). The line will enable the teacher to determine if Megan is progressing at the expected rate toward her goal. If Megan is progressing on target, the remaining WCPM data points will be close to the aim line.

4. *Continue collecting and graphing ORF data regularly.* Draw a phase-change line that shows when the intervention begins and continue collecting data as frequently as necessary (see Figure 2.1). Hosp et al. (2007) recommend that teachers administer ORF probes for struggling students once or twice each week. For higher-performing students, it is only necessary to collect data every other week or monthly. Within the RTI model, teachers should monitor the progress of students receiving Tier 3 instruction most frequently. Based on Megan's performance during baseline and the feasibility of classroom demands, the teacher decides to collect ORF CBM data for Megan on a weekly basis.

Making instructional decisions. In order to enhance the effectiveness of CBM, teachers must consistently employ decision rules when examining student data. Decision rules are guidelines for interpreting student progress. Wright (2001) recommends the three-data-point rule. Using this method of analysis, teachers compare the student's CBM scores to the aim line. If the data points are clustered close to the aim line, above and below, no change of instruction is needed because the student is progressing at the expected rate. If three consecutive data points are above the aim line, the end goal should be raised to reflect a more ambitious rate of progress. If three consecutive data points fall below the aim line, instruction should be modified to increase student achievement. For example, students falling below their aim line may need supplemental small-group or one-on-one instruction.

When modifying instruction, draw another phase-change line and label the new phase. Figure 2.1 shows that during Tier 1 instruction, Megan's WCPM fell below the aim line on three consecutive sessions. So, her teacher made a decision to modify instruction. For Tier 2 instruction, Megan's teacher provided additional oral reading practice in small groups three times per week and began using a systematic error correction procedure during instruction. After implementing Tier 2 instruction, the number of Megan's WCPM increased to the expected rate when compared to the aim line.

CBM Maze

Obtaining materials. Maze is a curriculum-based measure of reading proficiency that requires students to read silently and comprehend what they read. Passages for Maze should consist of more than 300 words and every seventh word should be deleted. In place of each deleted word, there should be three choices in brackets from which the student will select the correct word. Teachers can create their own Maze probes using appropriately leveled reading passages. However, purchasing premade materials will help to ensure consistency of reading levels and save time. CBM Maze passages are available on AIMSweb for grades one through eight and Edcheckup for grades one through six (see Table 2.1). When administering the Maze, the teacher will also need a stop watch, the directions and script for administration, and the answer keys for scoring.

Administering and scoring Maze. Maze is more efficient than ORF CBM because it can be administered to the whole class at the same time. Each student should have a copy of a Maze passage face down on his or her desk. The teacher then reads the scripted directions that accompany the Maze materials. The directions should state that when the teacher gives the signal (says "Begin") the students will turn over the paper, read the passage silently, and circle or underline the correct word when they come to a group of three words in brackets. They are encouraged to work as quickly as possible. At the end of three minutes, the teacher tells the students to put their pencils down and turn their papers over. Then she collects the Maze passages for scoring. To obtain the CBM Maze score of Words Correctly Restored (WCR), total the number of responses attempted then subtract the number of errors.

Graph Maze data. Figure 2.2 shows an example of a CBM graph of WCR for Max, an eighth grader who is performing about average when compared to his peers. For the Maze graph, the vertical axis should show number of

Figure 2.2 CBM Maze Data for Max

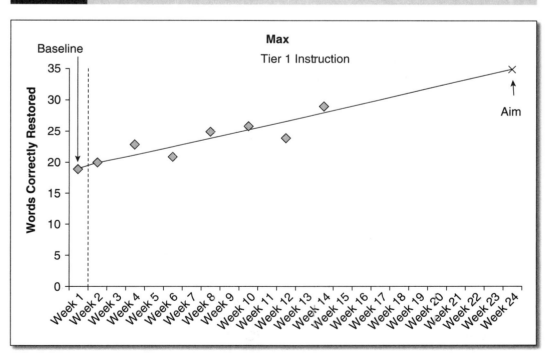

words correctly restored (WCR) and the horizontal axis will show each week until the end of the school (Week 1, Week 2, and so on).

1. *Collect and graph baseline data.* Similar to ORF, the students should complete three Maze passages on the first session. The median score of the three Maze passages will be the first data point on the graph. For example, Max scored 19 WCR on his first Maze, 18 on his second Maze, and 20 on his third Maze. Because his median score is 19, the teacher plots a 19 on Max's graph for his baseline data point. Then she draws a phase-change line.

2. *Set appropriate goals.* Max's median baseline score is 19 WCR, which is almost the fiftieth percentile for an eighth grader at the beginning of the school year (see the norm table for Maze on AIMSweb). The teacher determines that an appropriate goal for Max would be 35 WCR because that would place him slightly above the seventy-fifth percentile by spring when compared to other eighth graders on this measure. Ambitious goals for CBM Maze growth rates are about one WCR every two to three weeks (Fuchs & Fuchs, 2004).

3. *Draw an aim line.* Max's teacher then draws an aim line from the first data point (19) to the goal of 35 WCR by the end of the school year. If all of the subsequent CBM Maze scores are close to the line, Max will be showing expected progress toward his goal.

4. *Continue collecting and graphing CBM data regularly.* Determine the frequency of data collection based upon individual students' level of proficiency. Because Max is performing on grade level, his teacher decides to administer CBM Maze to him every two weeks to monitor his progress.

Making instructional decisions. Teachers can examine the graphed CBM Maze data using the same decision-making rules they use for oral reading fluency. That is, if the data points continue to ascend staying close to the aim line, the student is making expected progress and no change is necessary. If three consecutive data points are above the aim line, the end goal should be raised to reflect a more ambitious rate of progress. If three consecutive data points fall below the aim line, instruction should be modified to increase student achievement. Figure 2.2 shows that, under Tier 1 instruction, Max made steady progress toward his goal so no additional interventions were needed.

CBM Early Reading

Variations of CBM early reading are available for younger children. AIMSweb provides materials for assessing letter naming fluency, letter sound fluency, phoneme segmentation fluency, and nonsense word fluency. DIBELS also provides assessments for letter naming and nonsense word fluency, and assesses phoneme segmentation fluency and initial sound fluency as well. Hosp et al. (2007) recommend using letter sound fluency (LSF) and word identification fluency (WIF) to assess early reading performance for children in grades K–1.

When assessing letter sound fluency (LSF), provide students with a sheet of paper showing a series of isolated alphabet letters in random sequence and instruct the student to point to each letter and say the letter sound. Time the student for one minute while scoring the number of correct and incorrect responses. The LSF and WIF scores are calculated by counting the number of sounds or words attempted minus the total number of errors. The basic procedures for administration, scoring, graphing, and decision making for early CBM reading are the same as those described for ORF and Maze. CBM materials and directions for letter sound fluency and word identification fluency are available at Edcheckup, AIMSweb, and Intervention Central (see Table 2.1). Intervention Central also provides early reading assessments in Spanish.

VOCABULARY MATCHING

CBM can also be used to monitor progress in content areas using a procedure called vocabulary matching. Busch and Espin (2003) demonstrated that CBM vocabulary matching reliably predicts performance with science and social studies content on teacher-made tests and standardized achievement tests. This CBM can be administered to the whole class at the same time and requires students to match as many vocabulary words with their definitions in five minutes.

TeachingLD.org describes the following procedures for creating vocabulary-matching probes. Select vocabulary words that will be covered during the whole school year (from textbooks, lectures, assigned reading) and develop a short, clear definition for each word. Write the words and definitions on index cards. Then create weekly vocabulary-matching probes by shuffling the index cards and randomly selecting 20 vocabulary words per probe. Each probe will have 20 numbered vocabulary words listed on the left column of the page with a blank space next to each word. On the right column, there are 22 definitions with a letter next to each one. During administration, students have five minutes to match the definitions to the words by writing the letter that corresponds with the definition in the blank space next to the vocabulary word.

Vocabulary-matching probes may be administered once a week to the whole class. When providing directions, teachers should tell students they are not expected to finish and will see words they have not yet covered in class. After recording and graphing the number of correct responses, examine the data to monitor student progress in content areas. An appropriate expectation for rate of growth in vocabulary matching should be about one word per week. In addition to providing a brief measure of content-area achievement, this weekly assessment continuously exposes students to all of the content-area vocabulary they are studying throughout the school year. This repeated exposure is likely to help students maintain previously learned vocabulary. Additionally, on all subsequent content-area units, new vocabulary will already be familiar to the students, allowing for quicker learning.

Miscue Analysis and Comprehension Checks

Miscue analysis. In addition to using CBM reading to monitor overall reading proficiency, teachers may need additional diagnostic information to plan instruction for struggling readers. Miscue analysis is one way to obtain more information about specific areas of strength and weakness in oral reading and comprehension. As the teacher listens to a student reading a passage, she records and tallies each type of miscue (reading error). An analysis of miscues can help teachers find possible error patterns to target for instruction. The following are types of errors to record during timed oral reading:

- Omissions are recorded when a student skips a word.
- Insertions are recorded when a student adds a word not in the text.
- Reversals are recorded when a student says consecutive words in the wrong sequence.
- Substitutions are recorded when a student replaces a word in the text with a different word.
- Hesitations are recorded when a student does not say the word within three seconds, and the word needs to be supplied by the teacher.

There are several reading inventories that use miscue analysis to help teachers identify specific areas to target for instruction. For example, the *Analytical Reading Inventory (ARI)* (Woods & Moe, 2003) measures word recognition and comprehension and allows the assessor to record and analyze miscues to identify error patterns. In the *ARI*, the teacher calculates percentage of passage accuracy to determine independent, instructional, or frustration levels. Other reading inventories include *Basic Reading Inventory* (Johns, 2005), *Comprehensive Reading Inventory* (Cooter, Flynt, & Cooter, 2007), *Classroom Reading Inventory* (Wheelok, Campbell, & Silvaroli, 2008), and *English-Español Reading Inventory for the Classroom* (Flynt & Cooter, 1999).

Comprehension checks. Analytical inventories also allow teachers to obtain information about reading comprehension. Two ways to assess comprehension include asking questions about the reading passage or having the student orally retell the reading passage. To assess the student's level of comprehension teachers can ask literal, inferential, or critical comprehension questions (McKenna & Stahl, 2009). Literal comprehension questions require the student to recall information from the text that was stated explicitly, including the main idea and details, comparisons, and sequence of events. Inferential questions require students to comprehend information that was not explicitly stated, but implied. Making predictions and deducing cause-effect relationships are examples of inferential comprehension skills. Critical questions require students to make value judgments or express their opinions about a reading passage and support their opinions with logic or experience. Critical analysis questions may include questions about the quality of the reading passage, the author's intent, or whether or not the student agrees with the author's position (McKenna & Stahl).

Another way to assess comprehension is to have the student retell the reading passage immediately after reading. The teacher can prepare an answer sheet that lists all of the important details and facts from the reading passage and check off each detail as the student retells the story. In addition to assessing recall of story events, oral retelling may provide insight into the student's values and cultural influences (McKenna & Stahl, 2009). Additionally, oral retelling is recommended for English language learners because their language fluency can also be assessed along with their reading comprehension (Spinelli, 2008). When using oral retelling, teachers should be careful to not mistake oral expression limitations for inaccuracies in reading comprehension.

Authentic Assessment

Although CBM and informal diagnostic reading assessments are appropriate for most diverse learners, teachers may find it useful to supplement these assessments with more qualitative information. Spinelli (2008) recommends performance-based assessment and portfolio assessment for diverse learners. Performance-based assessments are designed to measure student achievement with authentic and meaningful tasks that often require students to integrate their language arts skills. Examples of performance assessment include interviews, simulations, debates, presentations, research projects, and role-plays (Pierce & O'Malley, 1992).

Performance-based assessments are more time consuming than CBM, but they supplement CBM data with a more complete picture of student performance. Many gifted students, typically developing students, and students with disabilities demonstrate asymmetrical development of academic and social skills. Through performance-based assessment, teachers can identify any number of specific strengths and talents including creativity, persistence, social skills, problem-solving skills, and the ability to analyze, synthesize, and apply information. Additionally, teachers can observe areas of weakness to target for instruction. Performance-based assessment is especially supportive of diverse learners, including English language learners, because it allows them to show growth with a variety of literacy, social, and content-area skills in a variety of authentic contexts (Spinelli, 2008).

Permanent products from these kinds of authentic assessments can be compiled into individual portfolios to provide qualitative information about a student's performance in reading. Portfolios can showcase the student's best work, document mastery of specific reading objectives, and show growth over the course of the school year. Because they provide a vivid picture of student performance, portfolios are also very useful for communicating with parents from all backgrounds.

SUMMARY

Accurate screening and monitoring of reading proficiency is necessary for planning appropriate and differentiated instruction for diverse learners. In order to make effective instructional decisions in the inclusive classroom, teachers must continuously monitor the progress of all students. Struggling students will need their progress monitored more frequently than higher-performing students so teachers can make timely decisions about the type and intensity of instruction needed. Research demonstrates that CBM reading is a valid, reliable, and efficient way to continuously monitor the progress of every student. Two ways to monitor overall reading proficiency include oral reading fluency and Maze. Oral reading fluency is assessed by having the student read a passage for one minute and counting the number of words correct per minute (WCPM). Maze requires students to read a passage silently for three minutes and supply the correct missing word from a choice of three to determine the number of words correctly restored (WCR). CBM can also be used to monitor early reading skills such as letter sound fluency, phoneme segmentation fluency, and word identification fluency. Teachers can examine CBM data to determine appropriate individualized goals and then create simple graphs that show the extent to which students are making progress toward their goals. Although CBM is a quick and direct method for continuously monitoring overall reading progress, teachers will likely need to supplement CBM with additional diagnostic information to identify specific areas of strength and weakness. Teachers can use miscue analysis and informal comprehension checks to supplement CBM information. Teachers can also include performance-based and portfolio assessment to gain a more complete picture of student capabilities.

MAYA

"Maya, it's your turn to read." Ms. Kelsey, the special education inclusion teacher, was conducting CBM reading for the third graders who needed their progress monitored on a weekly basis. Maya put her pencil down on her vocabulary worksheet, bounced over to Ms. Kelsey, sat down in the seat across from her, and beamed. Maya always enjoyed one-on-one attention from her teachers.

"Hello Maya. You're in a good mood!"

"I'm going to read really well today!" Maya knew she was becoming a better reader because of the chart Ms. Kelsey showed her every week. She was also getting very good at answering the comprehension questions Ms. Kelsey asked her when she finished reading the stories.

"Well, that's a good attitude!" Ms. Kelsey gave Maya a handout with a story printed on it and said, "OK, are you ready?" Maya nodded emphatically.

"OK." Ms. Kelsey read the brief standardized directions of the CBM aloud to Maya then said, "Begin." As Maya read the story about a snake named Sam and a lizard named Lilly, Ms. Kelsey followed along on her own copy, keeping track of the number and type of miscues. After one minute, Ms. Kelsey marked the last word Maya read, and let her finish reading the story. "Well done, Maya, I think you beat your last reading rate. Let's see." Ms. Kelsey was able to quickly determine the number of words read because her copy of the passage had the number of words totaled at the end of each line. "So, Maya, today you read 95 words in one minute, and you made five mistakes, so that's 90 correct words per minute."

"That's good, right? Put it on the chart!" Maya knew she beat her last score.

"OK." Ms. Kelsey took Maya's chart out of her folder and wrote a data point at 90 on Session 18. "Well, look—you beat your last score! What was it?"

Maya looked at the chart, put her finger on the last data point and said, "It was only 81, but it's 90 today!"

"That's nine more words than you read the last time. Look at all these data points on your chart. See, every time you read, you continue to improve and get closer to your goal."

"I know," Maya smiled, "I'm ready to answer the questions!"

"OK." Ms. Kelsey was delighted with Maya's enthusiasm. "Who were the main characters?"

"Sam and Lilly. They were best friends, they lived in a cage at the zoo."

"You're right! What was the problem?"

"Sam was jealous of Lilly because she was more colorful and got more attention, but Lilly didn't care about any of that. She just liked Sam the best."

After Maya finishes answering the comprehension questions, she springs back to her seat to finish her vocabulary worksheet. Before Ms. Kelsey calls the next student, she makes a note that Maya's literal reading comprehension is improving and her reading errors were mostly omissions of suffixes (such as clap instead of clapped, point instead of pointing). She plans to target suffixes for Maya during their Tier 2 reading instruction. She also plans to challenge Maya with more inferential reading comprehension questions.

3

Implementing Multitiered Reading Instruction

Reading is undeniably the most important skill for academic success in school and for independent functioning throughout adulthood. The ability to read is an indispensible tool for learning, performing functional tasks, and entertaining oneself. Reading proficiency has substantial impact on education and employment opportunities as well as independent functioning and quality of life. Each day as we live and work, we can expect to read signs, directions, labels, newspapers, notes, e-mails, books, menus, forms, magazines, electronic files, reports, letters, text messages, bills, and Web pages. Poor reading ability limits full participation in everyday events that proficient readers may take for granted.

Unfortunately, reading achievement has been and continues to be a challenge. According to the National Center for Education Statistics (2007), only about one third of all fourth and eighth graders scored at or above proficient in reading. Furthermore, only 13 percent to 17 percent of African American and Hispanic fourth and eighth graders scored at or above proficient. No Child Left Behind sets the goal of all children reading at or above grade level by third grade and mandates that teachers consider evidence-based practices when making instructional decisions. This chapter will present evidence-based practices for teaching reading to diverse learners in inclusive classrooms using various instructional arrangements within in a three-tiered Response to Intervention (RTI) model.

EVIDENCE-BASED PRACTICES

Effective teachers in inclusive classrooms understand the need for planning and implementing differentiated reading instruction based on accurate progress monitoring (Gersten et al., 2009). Evidenced-based reading programs in K–12 classrooms provide balanced instruction of decoding skills, fluency, vocabulary, and comprehension. In general, evidence-based early reading instruction includes direct instruction of basic reading skills including manipulating phonemes (segmenting, blending), applying letter-sound correspondence, decoding words fluently, and comprehending vocabulary (Kamps & Greenwood, 2005). Developing readers need direct instruction, modeling, and frequent practice opportunities with immediate and specific feedback. Additionally, readers of all ages need opportunities to apply new skills to authentic and varied reading tasks.

As developing readers become more adept with decoding, reading instruction will place more emphasis on building vocabulary and reading comprehension strategies. In addition to extra support with decoding skills, struggling readers need explicit instruction of reading comprehension strategies, frequent practice, and opportunities for extended discussion of text meaning (see Vaughn et al., 2008; Kamil et al., 2008). In addition to explicit instruction and frequent practice and feedback, English language learners also benefit significantly from intensive small-group instruction, extensive vocabulary instruction, and peer-mediated instruction (Gersten et al., 2007). Each of these factors must be considered when planning and delivering multitiered reading instruction. Table 3.1 shows examples of evidence-based commercial reading programs identified by *What Works Clearinghouse* that can be used with diverse learners within multitiered teaching arrangements.

Table 3.1 Examples of Evidence-Based Reading Programs Identified by the What Works Clearinghouse

Program	Contact	Suggested Tier	Grade Level	Evidence-Based Outcomes
Accelerated Reader (Computer-based Program)	Learning, Inc. PO Box 8036, Wisconsin Rapids WI 54495 www.renlearn.com/ar/	Tiers 1–3	Grades K–12	General reading achievement
Bilingual Cooperative Integrated Reading and Composition (BCIRC)	Success for All Foundation, Inc. 200 W. Towsontown Boulevard Baltimore, MD 21204-5200 www.successforall.org	Tier 2	Grades 2–5 ELL	Reading achievement and language development for ELL students
ClassWide Peer Tutoring-Learning Management System (CWPT-LMS)	Juniper Gardens Children's Project 650 Minnesota Avenue, 2nd floor Kansas City, KS 66101 www.jgcp.ku.edu	Tier 1	Grades K–6	General reading achievement
Corrective Reading	SRA/McGraw-Hill 220 East Danieldale Road Desoto, TX 75115-2490 http://www.sraonline.com	Tiers 2 & 3	Grades 3–12	Alphabetics and fluency

Program	Contact	Suggested Tier	Grade Level	Evidence-Based Outcomes
DaisyQuest (Computer-based Program)	Gina C. Erickson DaisyQuest@comcast.net	Tiers 2 & 3	Preschool to Grade 2	Alphabetics
Early Intervention in Reading	*Early Intervention in Reading* program *EIR* Professional Development Program c/o Ceil Critchley 11293 Hastings Street NE Blaine, MN 55449 www.earlyinterventioninreading.com	Tiers 1 & 2 for K–2 Tiers 2 & 3 for third and fourth grade	Grades K–4	Alphabetics and comprehension
Earobics (Computer-based Program)	Earobics | Houghton Mifflin Harcourt Learning Technology 222 Berkeley Street Boston, MA 02116 www.earobics.com	Tier 1 for younger Tiers 2 & 3 for older	Preschool to Grade 3	Alphabetics and fluency
Enhanced Proactive Reading	Vaughn Gross Center for Reading and Language Arts College of Education SZB 228, University of Texas at Austin 1 University Station D4900 Austin, TX 78712 www.texasreading.org/utcrla/	Tier 2	Grade 1 ELL	Reading achievement of ELL students
Fast ForWord (Computer-based Program)	Scientific Learning 300 Frank H. Ogawa Plaza, Suite 600 Oakland, CA 94612-2040 http://www.scilearn.com	Tiers 1–3	K–3	Alphabetics
Instructional Conversations and Literature Logs	Center for Research on Education Diversity & Excellence (CREDE) Graduate School of Education 1640 Tolman Hall University of California Berkeley, CA 94720-1670 http://crede.berkeley.edu	Tier 2	Grades 2–5	Reading achievement and language development of ELL students
Kaplan SpellRead	Kaplan, Inc. and its Kaplan K12 Learning Services Division 1 Liberty Plaza, 22nd Floor New York, NY 10006 http://kaplank12.com/	Tiers 2–3	Grades 2–12	Alphabetics, fluency, and comprehension
Ladders to Literacy	Brookes Publishing Co. P.O. Box 10624 Baltimore, MD 21285-0624 www.brookespublishing.com	Tiers 1–3	Kindergarten	Alphabetics and fluency
LIPS Lindamood Phonemic Sequencing	416 Higuera Street San Luis Obispo, CA 93401 http://www.lindamoodbell.com	Tiers 2–3	Grades K–3	Alphabetics
Peer-Assisted Learning Strategies (PALS)	Vanderbilt University Attn: Flora Murray/PALS Orders Box 328 Peabody Nashville, TN 37203-5701 http://kc.vanderbilt.edu/pals/	Tier 1	Grades K–12	Alphabetics, fluency, and comprehension; Reading achievement of ELL students

(Continued)

Table 3.1 (Continued)

Program	Contact	Suggested Tier	Grade Level	Evidence-Based Outcomes
Reading Recovery	Reading Recovery Council of North America (RRCNA) 400 West Wilson Bridge Road, Suite 250 Worthington, OH 43085-5218 http://www.readingrecovery.org	Tier 3	Grade 1	General reading achievement
Read Well	Sopris West 4093 Specialty Place Longmont, CO 80504 http://store.cambiumlearning.com/	Tiers 1–3	Grades K–1	Reading achievement of ELL students
SRA Reading Mastery	SRA/McGraw Hill 220 East Danieldale Road DeSoto, TX 75115-2490 www.sraonline.com	Tiers 1–2	Grades K–6	Reading achievement of ELL students
Steppingstones to Literacy	Sopris West 4093 Specialty Place Longmont, CO 80504 www.sopriswest.com	Tiers 1–3	Kindergarten	Alphabetics
Success for All	Success for All Foundation, Inc. 200 W. Towsontown Boulevard, Baltimore, MD 21204 www.successforall.net	Tier 1	Preschool to Grade 8	Alphabetics and general reading achievement
SuccessMaker (Computer-based Program)	Pearson Digital Learning. One Lake Street Upper Saddle River NJ 07458 www.pearsoned.com	Tiers 2–3	Grades K–8	Comprehension and general reading achievement
Vocabulary Improvement Program for English Language Learners and Their Classmates (VIP)	Brookes Publishing Co. PO Box 10624 Baltimore, MD 21285-0624 www.brookespublishing.com/store/ books/lively-6342/index.htm	Tier 1	Grades 4–6	Reading achievement and language development for ELL students
Waterford Early Reading Program (Computer-based Program)	Pearson Digital Learning 6710 East Camelback Road Scottsdale, AZ 85251 http://www.pearsondigital.com/waterford	Tiers 1–3	Grades K–2	Alphabetics
Wilson Reading System	Wilson Language Training 47 Old Webster Road Oxford, MA 01540 www.wilsonlanguage.com/w_wrs.htm	Tiers 2–3	Grades 2–12	Alphabetics

READING INSTRUCTION: TIER 1

Tier 1 reading programs include whole-class instruction and differentiated instruction in small, homogeneous groups. Regardless of group size, students should be making academic responses to instruction as frequently as possible. The following are Tier 1 evidence-based practices for increasing active student responding for reading instruction.

Choral responding. Choral responding is having the whole class make a simultaneous verbal response to a question or prompt. Choral responding is most effective when teachers present instruction at a lively pace with a clear signal for each response (for example, "What word?" or snap fingers) and immediate feedback (praise, error correction [Heward, 1994]). Questions or prompts designed for choral responding activities should have only one correct answer that is short (one to three words). Choral responding is the primary mode of active student responding in evidence-based direct instruction reading programs (such as *SRA Reading Mastery, Corrective Reading*). Teachers can use choral responding activities to teach phonemic awareness ("Say the beginning sound in the word *hat*."), decoding skills ("Let's sound out this word together. /h/ /a/ /t/."), vocabulary skills ("What is a synonym for *happy?*), reading fluency (choral reading), and reading comprehension ("Who is the main character?").

Response cards. Students can actively respond to instruction using individual dry-erase boards and markers or preprinted response cards (such as signs with the answers printed on them). Similar to choral responding, all students can answer questions simultaneously. Research demonstrates that using response cards substantially increases student achievement, participation, and on-task behavior (Heward, 1994; Randolph, 2007). Response cards can be used to practice a range of reading skills. For phonics instruction, teachers can pronounce a word and have students write the initial, medial, or final sounds. For vocabulary instruction, students can write the correct word in response to a teacher-read definition. Students can also write the answers to comprehension questions.

To increase responses and accommodate students with writing difficulties, teachers can use preprinted response cards that display a series of letters or words. Students can hold up the correct letter or word card when prompted ("Hold up the word *said*."). For reading comprehension, the teacher can read a series of statements about a passage and have students respond to each statement by holding up the correct sign (true or false, fact or opinion, agree or disagree). As with choral responding, teachers should provide immediate feedback after each response and end each trial with the students producing the correct answer (Heward, 1994).

Guided notes. When using guided notes, teachers provide an outline of the lecture with prompts (bullets, numbers, blank lines) for students to write down the important information as it is presented. Guided notes help students stay focused on the lesson by allowing them to actively respond to instruction, identify key information, and create an accurate and complete study guide (Heward, 1994). For example, guided notes can be used to teach different text structures (such as narrative, expository), reading comprehension strategies, or vocabulary words. Guided notes can also be modified for students who have writing challenges. Figure 3.1 shows an example of two different versions of guided notes for teaching content-area vocabulary words. The modified version (Form B) requires less writing and allows struggling students to keep up with the rest of the class during large-group instruction. Both versions can be used simultaneously during the same lesson. Struggling students should also be paired with a buddy to review their guided notes together, checking for accuracy and completeness.

| Figure 3.1 | Examples of Guided Notes |

Guided Notes: Form A

Arthropods (means "jointed feet"): Invertebrate animals with an exoskeleton and jointed limbs
- *Invertebrates are animals with no backbone.*
- *Exoskeleton is an external skeleton that protects the animal (like armor).*
  Three Kinds of Arthropods: *insects, arachnids, and crustaceans*

Insects: 3 body segments, 6 legs, 2 antennae
- Examples: *grasshoppers, beetles, butterflies, flies, bees, ants*

Arachnids: 2 body segments, 8 legs, no antennae
- Examples: *spiders, scorpions, ticks*

Crustaceans: 3 body segments; diversity of legs, claws, antennae; most are aquatic
- Examples: *lobsters, shrimp, crabs, krill*

For Homework: Draw and label the parts of each kind of arthropod.

Insect	Arachnid	Crustacean

Guided Notes: Form B

Arthropods (means "jointed feet"): Invertebrate animals with an exoskeleton and jointed limbs
- Invertebrates are animals with no <u>backbone</u>.
- Exoskeleton is an external skeleton that protects the animal (<u>like armor</u>).
  Three Kinds of Arthropods: *insects, arachnids, and crustaceans*

Insects: 3 body segments, 6 legs, 2 antennae
- Examples: grasshoppers, beetles, butterflies, <u>flies, bees, ants</u>

Arachnids: 2 body segments, 8 legs, no antennae
- Examples: <u>spiders,</u> scorpions, ticks

Crustaceans: 3 body segments; diversity of legs, claws, antennae; most are aquatic
- Examples: lobsters, shrimp, <u>crabs,</u> <u>krill</u>

For Homework: Draw one of each arthropod and write what kind it is.

Insect	Arachnid	Crustacean

Peer-mediated instruction. Classwide peer tutoring and cooperative learning groups are peer-mediated instructional arrangements that increase active student responding, achievement, and opportunities to practice social skills. Additionally, research demonstrates that diverse learners, especially ELL students, make the greatest academic gains when they participate in peer-mediated instruction (see Crandall, Jaramillo, Olsen, & Peyton, 2001; Snowman & Biehler, 2003). Peer-Assisted Learning Strategies (PALS) and Classwide Peer Tutoring-Learning Management System (CWPT-LMS) are examples of evidence-based reading programs that include reciprocal peer-mediated practice activities for decoding words, spelling, recalling vocabulary definitions, reading continuous text, and answering comprehension questions. Peer-mediated programs are highly structured and require students to learn procedures for delivering response prompts, error correction, and praise.

READING INSTRUCTION: TIERS 2 AND 3

Most of the students not making adequate progress in Tier 1 can achieve success with the more intensive Tier 2 interventions. Tier 2 interventions provide supplemental instruction to small groups of students experiencing the same kinds of skill difficulties. Vaughn and Roberts (2007) identify several key elements of effective Tier 2 reading interventions. These include providing direct and systematic instruction with frequent practice and ongoing feedback to similar ability groups, using reading materials at the appropriate reading level, providing ample opportunities for students to apply and practice new skills, requiring students to write, and monitoring student progress frequently to guide decisions about instruction and grouping. If students are not responding adequately to Tier 2 instruction, they should be engaged in additional instruction that targets specific reading skills. For Tier 3 instruction, Gersten and colleagues (2009) recommend teachers modify the pace of instruction, arrange several intensive one-on-one sessions daily, and provide frequent practice with high-quality feedback.

Research also demonstrates that the most effective reading programs at all three tiers provide explicit instruction in the following component reading skills: phonemic awareness, alphabetic principle, fluency, vocabulary, and comprehension (National Reading Panel, 2000). Balanced reading instruction combines these five skills, placing more emphasis in different areas as needed by individual learners. The following are strategies for teaching the reading components within a multitiered model.

PHONEMIC AWARENESS: TIER 1

Phonemic awareness, an essential skill for learning to read, is the most accurate predictor of future reading success (NRP, 2000). Phonemic awareness is the ability to discriminate and manipulate individual sounds in spoken words and includes skills such as rhyming words, counting syllables, isolating sounds, and segmenting and blending sounds. Effective phonemic awareness training is explicit, focused, logically sequenced, and delivered in brief instructional sessions (10–15 minutes). Vaughn and Linan-Thompson (2004) make the following suggestions for teaching phonemic awareness:

- Determine target phonemic awareness skills for large- and small-group instruction.
- Model the skill and provide practice (Teacher: "Watch me and listen. I'm going to say the sounds in the word *bat* separately. The sounds in bat are /b/ /a/ /t/." After modeling, the teacher says, "Together, *bat*, /b/ /a/ /t/." The students and teacher segment the word together, then the teacher says "Now, your turn, *bat*." The students segment the word as a group without the teacher.).
- Use body movements or manipulatives to add visibility to oral tasks ("Watch me, I'm going to hold up a finger for each sound in *bat*, /b/ /a/ /t/. Now we'll do it together."). Other examples include taking a step for each sound, clapping hands, snapping fingers, moving markers placed on desks, or writing slash marks on a dry-erase board.
- Provide frequent response opportunities with contingent praise and corrective feedback as needed. When students are responding, whether in large groups, small groups, or individually, teachers must listen for errors. If an error is made, the teacher models the correct answer, repeats the learning trial, and provides praise when students respond correctly. Brief phonemic awareness training sessions can be conducted in connection with ongoing activities throughout the day ("It's time to line up to go to lunch. What is the first sound in the word *lunch?* What is the first sound in the word *line?*).
- Phonemic awareness activities should be sequenced from easiest to most difficult.

When planning the sequence of instruction, teachers should consider that words with fewer phonemes are easier to segment, and phonemes at the beginning of a word are easier to segment than middle and end phonemes (Vaughn & Linan-Thompson, 2004). Yopp and Yopp (2000) recommend teaching the following sequence of phonemic awareness skills: rhyming, syllable manipulation, onset and rime, phoneme manipulation, and segmenting and blending. Segmenting and blending are the most important phonemic awareness skills for teaching children to read (NRP, 2000). Bursuck and Damer (2007) recommend the following teaching sequence for segmenting and blending phonemes:

1. Segment the first sound. The teacher says a word and the students identify the first sound (Teacher: "Say the first sound in *pen*." Students: "/p/.").

2. Blend onset and rime. The teacher slowly says the beginning sound (onset) and then the rest of the word (rime). Then the students say the whole word (Teacher: "Listen, /s/—/it/. What word?" Students: "Sit.").

3. Segment onset and rime. The teacher says the whole word and prompts the students to say the separate onset and rime parts (Teacher: "Break apart *dog*." Students: "/d/—/og/.").

4. Blend individual sounds. The teacher slowly says each individual sound in a word and the students say the whole word (Teacher: "I'll say the sounds, you put them together, /p/ /l/ /a/ /y/. What word?" Students: "Play.")

5. Segment individual sounds. The teacher says the word and the students say each sound (Teacher: "Break apart the word *last*." Students: "/l/ /a/ /s/ /t/.").

In addition to being direct and systematic, phonemic awareness activities for young readers should be interactive, engaging, and fun (Vaughn & Roberts, 2007; Yopp, 1992). To be most effective, phonemic awareness training should be connected to meaningful context such as stories, songs, poems, or thematic units (Edelen-Smith, 1997). When connecting literature with phonemic awareness instruction, teachers should point out language use and encourage students to identify and predict sounds, words, and sentences (Yopp & Yopp, 2000). For example, teachers can use the poem "Boa Constrictor" by Shel Silverstein (1974) and have students perform actions while identify rhyming words. The poem begins "Oh I'm being eaten by a boa constrictor, A boa constrictor, A boa constrictor, I'm being eaten by a boa constrictor, And I don't like it—one bit." As they recite the rest of the poem, have the students perform the following actions:

- "Well, what do you know? It's nibblin' my toe." *Have the students touch their toes.*
- "Oh, gee, it's up to my knee." *Have the students touch their knees.*
- "Oh my, it's up to my thigh." *Have the students touch their thighs.*
- "Oh, fiddle, it's up to my middle." *Have the students touch their waists.*
- "Oh, heck, it's up to my neck." *Have the students touch their necks.*
- "Oh, dread, it's upmmmmmmmmmmmmffffffffff." *Have the students cover their mouths with their hands.*

When they finish reciting the poem, prompt the students to identify the rhyming words in the poem as well as additional rhyming words ("What word in the poem rhymes with *know?*" "What else rhymes with *know* and *toe?*").

When students become more proficient with manipulating sounds, they can begin making connections to print. For example, students can write corresponding letters on their dry-erase boards as the teacher says each phoneme of a word during a segmenting activity. Another activity is giving students a bag with individual letters printed on index cards. The students put their letters at the top of their desks and move the letters to identify letter sounds, spell words, or make new words (Vaughn & Linan-Thompson, 2004).

Evidence-based commercial reading programs present phonemic awareness skills in a logical sequence and combine them with meaningful literacy activities (see Table 3.1). *Early Intervention Reading (EIR)* is an example of a reading program that can be used for Tier 1 instruction for K–2 students. *EIR* is designed for whole-class instruction with additional small-group supplemental instruction as needed. In kindergarten, students listen to stories and participate in creative dramatics to practice rhyming words, segmenting and blending sounds, and identifying letters and sounds. In first and second grade, students continue with phonemic awareness and phonics instruction along with repeated story reading, guided sentence writing, vocabulary instruction, and comprehension instruction. For third and fourth graders, *EIR* can be used for Tiers 2 or 3 reading instruction.

PHONEMIC AWARENESS: TIERS 2 AND 3

In general, students in kindergarten through first grade who have a reading rate of at least 20 words per minute will not need additional phonemic awareness instruction (Vaughn & Linan-Thompson, 2004). However, students not responding adequately to Tier 1 instruction should be provided with more intensive phonemic awareness intervention for about 15–20 extra minutes per day. Supplementary phonemic awareness instruction has been demonstrated to be effective for young children, ELL students, students with disabilities, and students at risk for reading failure (NRP, 2000). These students benefit from additional small-group or one-on-one instruction and practice. Variations of the following rhyming, counting, and phoneme manipulation activities are recommended by Bursuck and Damer (2007), Edelen-Smith (1997), and Vaughn and Linan-Thompson (2004).

Rhyming. Students can listen to pairs of words and identify whether or not they rhyme (face/place; look/time), or select from three pictures the two that rhyme (pictures of a man, a fan, and a car). Reading rhyming books by Dr. Seuss (*Green Eggs and Ham, The Cat in the Hat, Fox in Socks, There's a Wocket in My Pocket*) and having students identify and practice rhyming words can be a motivating activity for additional phonemic awareness practice.

Counting words, syllables, and phonemes. Teachers can select a series of sentences (maybe from a favorite story), read a sentence, have the student tally each word as it is read, and report the total number of words in the sentences. Once students are able to count words in sentences, have them progress to counting syllables in words, and then counting phonemes in words. Using students' names for syllable and phoneme counting can increase interest in the activity. Students can count words, syllables, and phonemes by clapping hands, snapping fingers, slapping their legs, tapping the desk, or taking steps.

Phoneme manipulation. Provide direct instruction and frequent practice with sound isolation and segmentation ("What is the first sound in the word *house?*" "Say the sounds you hear in the word *seat.*"). Use interesting pictures or stories for motivation. For example, teachers can show pictures of different animals and prompt students to identify sounds in the animal words. Students can also practice identifying new words when phonemes are added or deleted ("The word is *pat*. What word would it be if you took away the *p*" or "The word is *it*, what word would it be if we add an *s* to the beginning?"). Students can also listen for similarities and differences in word phonemes and identify the word that does not belong (kitchen, father, kangaroo, keep). This activity can also be done with rhyming words (day, say, may, book). Yopp (1992) has adapted the song "If You're Happy and You Know It" to help students practice blending phonemes. Instead of singing, "If you're happy and you know it, clap your hands," the students sing, "If you think you know this word, shout it out!" (p. 700). Then teacher segments a word (/m/-/a/-/p/) and prompts the students to say the blended word (map).

In order to implement Tiers 2 and 3 phonemic awareness instruction for older students and English language learners, teachers should use culturally relevant, age-appropriate materials for instruction and practice. McQuiston, O'Shea, and McCollin (2008) recommend using hip-hop music, culturally specific word games, and multicultural poetry to support phonemic awareness development.

Examples of evidence-based commercial reading programs that can be used for phonemic awareness instruction in Tiers 2 and 3 include *Lindamood Phonemic Sequencing (LIP), DaisyQuest,* and *Enhanced Proactive Reading* (see Table 3.1). *Lindamood Phonemic Sequencing (LIPS)* is a reading program designed for students in grades K–3. In this program, teachers help students become aware of the mouth movements that produce specific speech sounds. Students learn to check sounds within words and make self-corrections in speech, reading, and spelling.

DaisyQuest is an individualized computer software program targeting phonological awareness for young children (ages 3–7). Students practice beginning reading skills in the context of a fairy tale featuring Daisy, a friendly dragon. Activities include recognizing rhyming words, identifying words with the same sounds (initial, medial, and final), counting the number of sounds in words, and recognizing words that can be formed from separate phonemes.

Enhanced Proactive Reading is an evidence-based program determined to be effective for ELL students. *Enhanced Proactive Reading* is a comprehensive literacy program for first-grade English language learners with reading difficulties. The program is designed for small-group daily instruction with frequent opportunities for participation and feedback. Activities include playing phonemic awareness word games, practicing letter-sound correspondence, and writing alphabet letters.

ALPHABETIC PRINCIPLE: TIER 1

Alphabetic principle, the correspondence between phonemes (individual sounds) and their symbols (printed letters), is necessary for sounding out and decoding words. Alphabetic principle is most effectively taught using phonics instruction (NRP, 2000). For Tier 1 instruction, students need to learn letter-sound correspondence, regular-word reading, irregular-word reading, and reading in decodable text. Carnine, Silbert, Kame'enui, and Tarver (2004) and Bursuck and Damer (2007) recommend the following procedures for teaching letter-sound correspondence. The teacher introduces each new sound by writing the letter on the board or chart paper and using the following verbal sequence: (a) "My turn. This letter says /m/. What sound? /m/," (b) "Together, what sound? /m/," (teacher and students say the sound together), (c) "Your turn, what sound?" (students say the sound without the teacher and receive immediate feedback). Students respond when the teacher gives a signal.

The signal for continuous sounds (such as /s/, /m/, /n/, /f/, /l/, /r/, /h/) is pointing to the left of the letter, looping your finger under the letter and holding it for 2-seconds while modeling the sound, then looping your finger back to the starting point (Carnine et al., 2004; Bursuck & Damer, 2007). The signal for stop sounds (such as /b/, /d/, /g/, /k/, /g/, /j/, /p/, /t/) is looping to the letter from the starting point, bouncing your finger out as you model the sound, and returning to the starting point (Carnine et al.; Bursuck & Damer). Teachers should present several learning trials of a few letters at a time with positive and systematic feedback. If students make an error, begin the learning trial again starting with "My turn." Provide frequent and brief opportunities to practice letter-sound correspondence throughout the day. Start by teaching a few letter sounds that can be made into words. Then students can immediately apply the alphabetic principle to decoding meaningful print (Carnine et al.). For example, after teaching the letter sounds /m/, /p/, /s/, /t/, and /a/, teachers can combine those letters to teach students to sound out the following words: *at, mat, sat, pat, map, tap,* and so on. During initial instruction of new letters, teachers should not simultaneously introduce letters that look or sound too similar (for instance *b* and *d; m* and *n*).

As soon as students have learned six to eight letter-sound correspondences, teachers can begin instruction with sounding out regular words. When modeling and providing practice with sounding out words, teachers should use the "My Turn/Together/Your Turn" sequence and the same finger signals described above for continuous and stop sounds. For example, when sounding out the word *sat,* the teacher loops her finger to the /s/ and holds that sound for two seconds, loops to the /a/ and holds it for two seconds, and then loops to the /t/ and bounces it out while saying the stop sound /t/. After modeling sounding out the word, the teacher says, "What word? *Sat!*"

Vaughn and Linen-Thompson (2004) recommend the following sequence for teaching students to decode regular words. Begin teaching decoding skills with words having a short vowel-consonant (VC) pattern (at, it). Then teach CVC words (sit, mat), then blends (st, bl), and diagraphs (ph, sh). After teaching short vowel sounds, teach long vowel sounds, then variant vowels (ei) and dipthongs (oi). Select words for instruction that are familiar and appear frequently in authentic reading tasks.

Many high-frequency words in the English language are irregular and cannot be decoded phonetically (such as *said, of, was*). Because the sounds in irregular words do not completely correspond to their letter sounds, direct instruction of irregular words teaches students to spell the word instead of sounding it out. For example, the teacher writes the word on the board and says, "This word is *said.* What word? *Said.* Spell *said: S-a-i-d.*" Teachers should select irregular words for instruction based on the frequency of appearance in reading passages (Vaughn & Linan-Thompson, 2004). Previously taught irregular words (or sight words) should be reviewed daily and, along with regular words, should be practiced in the context of decodable text. Decodable text refers to leveled books with controlled vocabulary such as *SRA Phonics* (SRA/McGraw-Hill), *Scholastic Phonics* (Scholastic, Inc.), or *Phonics Readers* (Steck-Vaughn).

The next step is teaching students to use structural analysis to decode words. This requires instruction on word structures such as root words, prefixes, suffixes, compound words, and syllabication. When decoding more complex words, students can examine the word parts to figure them out. Vaughn et al. (2006) provide the following suggestions for teaching structural analysis:

- Teach meanings of words parts (*un* means *not; pre* means *before*).
- Demonstrate how big words are smaller words with prefixes and endings (*unbelievable* consists of *un, believe, able*).
- Show students how to decode words by covering different sections of the word and having them read the part of the word that is visible.
- Create word charts showing variations of one root word (happy, unhappy, happiness, lone, alone, lonely, loneliness).
- Make a class dictionary or wall chart that shows prefixes and suffixes and what they mean.

In order to be proficient with decoding, students need frequent opportunities for practice and application. Teachers can use a large bulletin board to create a "word wall" in which new words are added each week. As each new word is added, the teacher models the pronunciation and spelling, discusses the meaning, provides an example of the word in context, and leads students to generate sentences using the word. The word wall can be used as a reference tool for student reading or writing. Additionally, teachers can regularly review the words posted on the word wall using a quick drill (for instance, pointing to each word in random order, prompting choral responses, and providing immediate feedback). Students can also work in peer-tutoring dyads or cooperative learning groups to practice reading words, sorting words, or making new words.

SRA Reading Mastery can be used as a Tier 1 reading program in which students are provided with differentiated instruction at their reading levels determined by program placement assessments. *What Works Clearinghouse* identified *SRA Reading Mastery* as an evidence-based practice for improving the reading achievement of ELL students. This direct instruction program includes systematic phonics instruction as one part of a comprehensive reading package for students in grades K–6. *SRA Reading Mastery* uses a series of fast-paced interactive activities systematically designed and sequenced for teaching phonemic awareness, sound-letter correspondence, word and passage reading, vocabulary development, comprehension, and oral reading fluency. If teachers do not use *SRA Reading Mastery* for the whole class, this program can be used for students receiving Tiers 2 and 3 interventions.

ALPHABETIC PRINCIPLE: TIERS 2 AND 3

Teachers can use the same Tier 1 activities for instruction in Tiers 2 and 3 by providing more practice in small groups or one-on-one teaching arrangements. The following are phonics activities, or variations of activities, presented by Vaughn et al. (2006) and Vaughn and Linan-Thompson (2004) that can be used for Tiers 2 and 3 interventions:

- *Making words.* Provide students with manipulative letters (such as tiles, index cards, magnetic letters) and show them how new words are formed by moving the letters around. Have students practice reading a series of similar words (words with the same ending), then have students rearrange letters to form their own words.

- *Sorting words.* Provide pairs of students with several index cards with words printed on them, and have students work together to sort words with similar patterns.
- *Onset and rime piles.* Pairs of students can be provided with index cards that show onset letters in one pile (such as *d, p, m, r, s, t*) and ending rimes in another pile (-*at*, -*an*, -*in*, -*ake*, -*ink*). Students can work together to make words by matching onset cards with rime cards, and write down all of the new words that make sense.
- *File-folder games.* Teachers can make game boards and stacks of word cards. Students draw a card and advance their game piece the number of spaces indicated on the word card when they read a word correctly. Bingo games can also be used to practice decoding sight words.

Students can also benefit from fluency training with sight words. Each student can have an individualized set of word cards kept in a personalized box. Students can practice reading their words as quickly as possible during one-minute timed trials and self-graph their sight word fluency.

Strategy instruction is an evidence-based practice for older students who struggle with decoding. Lenz, Schumaker, Deshler, and Beals (1984) recommend the DISSECT strategy for adolescents with learning disabilities. The mnemonic DISSECT stands for the following word attack procedures: **D**iscover the word's context, **I**solate the prefix, **S**eparate the suffix, **S**ay the stem, **E**xamine the stem (pronounce the word, reread the whole sentence), **C**heck with someone, and **T**ry the dictionary. Before students use this strategy independently, the teacher discusses and models the strategy and provides guided practice.

Examples of evidence-based reading programs appropriate for instruction in Tiers 2 and 3 include *Wilson Reading System* and *Fast ForWord* (see Table 3.1). *Wilson Reading System* is a K–12 program designed to teach reading and spelling skills to students struggling most at the word level. This program includes instruction in phonemic awareness, letter-sound correspondence, sight words, fluency, vocabulary, oral expression, and comprehension. *Fast ForWord* is an individualized computer-based reading program for K–3 students. This program focuses on phonological awareness, beginning word recognition, and English language conventions. Students listen to instructions and feedback through headphones and respond using the computer mouse. Based on student responses, the software adapts to individual skill levels and adjusts content difficulty to increase the likelihood of correct responding.

FLUENCY: TIER 1

Fluent readers demonstrate proficiency when they read printed materials quickly, accurately, and with appropriate expression (NRP, 2000). Reading fluency is necessary for reading comprehension. When students are able to read fluently, they can focus more on the meaning of the text. The most effective way to increase reading fluency is providing frequent opportunities for students to read extended text. The following are examples of fluency-building activities:

- *Partner reading.* Pairs of students take turns reading a story, paragraph by paragraph or page by page. As one student reads, the other student monitors for errors. Students are taught a procedure for providing error correction and praise to each other. For example, if a student miscues a word, the reading partner says the word correctly, prompts the student to reread the sentence, and provides praise for reading the miscued word correctly. It is best to pair higher- and lower-performing students together, with the higher-performing student reading the passage first.
- *Partner reading plus.* Vaughn and Linen-Thompson (2004) recommend the following additions to partner reading: (a) partner reading plus a comprehension check (that is, students ask each other *who, what, when, where,* and *why* questions after they read the passage), (b) partner reading plus retelling (students practice comprehension by telling the story back to each other after they read it), and (c) partner reading plus graphing (students administer three one-minute timed readings to each other and graph their best reading rates).
- *Choral reading.* Students can also increase their reading fluency by participating in whole-class or small-group choral reading. Choral reading can occur throughout the school day during language arts and content-area instruction. For example, students can chorally read from their science and social studies text books.
- *Readers theater.* This activity involves frequent repeated readings of plays over the course of a week in preparation for a performance when students will read their parts to the class. In addition to increasing fluency, this activity helps students practice reading with proper expression. Struggling readers should have big reading parts because they need more practice.

Peer-Assisted Learning Strategies (PALS) is a K–12 Tier 1 reading program that has been identified as evidenced-based for increasing reading fluency, alphabetics, and comprehension for all students, and overall reading achievement for ELL students. The PALS program consists of structured activities including partner reading with retell, paragraph shrinking (stop at the end of each paragraph, identify the main idea and most important details, and state it in 10 words or less), and prediction relay (make predictions prior to reading each half page, confirm or disconfirm them, and summarize the main idea). The whole class participates in PALS for 35-minute sessions three days each week.

FLUENCY: TIERS 2 AND 3

Students struggling with reading fluency need additional opportunities for practice and systematic error correction. To achieve the best results, students should engage in repeated readings with appropriately leveled reading materials each day for brief timed sessions as a supplement to

Tier 1 reading instruction. Prior to having the student read the passage, use a brief comprehension strategy to improve performance. For example, activate prior knowledge by having the student look at the title and make predictions about the content. Then read the first two sentences to check, revise, and make further predictions (Alber-Morgan, Ramp, Anderson, & Martin, 2007). Prior to engaging in the timed reading, have students read through the passage once and provide systematic error correction for each miscued word (provide the correct word, have student repeat the word, and reread the sentence). Prior to having the students reread the passage, review the miscued words. At the end of each session, provide performance feedback by comparing the current reading rate to the previous reading rate ("You read 78 words per minute today, that's 8 more than yesterday!"). The following are additional activities for small-group and one-on-one instruction for improving reading fluency:

- *Listening passage preview.* The student follows along silently as the teacher reads the entire passage aloud. Then the student reads the passage aloud, receiving corrective feedback as needed (Wright, 2001).
- *Paired reading.* The teacher and student select a book and read chorally together until the child signals when he wants to read solo. The student continues reading aloud until he makes an error, at which point the teacher provides the correct word. Then teacher and student read the sentence together and continue reading chorally until the student signals again that he wants to read alone (McKenna & Stahl, 2009).
- *Echo reading.* The teacher reads a passage aloud one sentence or paragraph at a time while the student follows along reading silently. After each sentence (or paragraph), the student reads that section back to the teacher (McKenna & Stahl, 2009).
- *Taped reading.* The student practices reading a passage along with a tape recording of the passage until he can read the passage fluently.

Corrective Reading is example of an evidence-based Tiers 2 or 3 commercial reading program that increases reading fluency. This direct instruction program is designed for students in Grades 3–12 to promote decoding, fluency, and comprehension skills for struggling readers. An evidence-based computer program that increases reading fluency is *Earobics*. Students in prekindergarten through third grade can respond to animated characters to build phonemic awareness, phonics skills, and language skills required for comprehension. The software package includes audiocassettes, videotapes, picture/word cards, big books, little books, and leveled readers for reading independently or in groups.

VOCABULARY: TIER 1

A critical skill for reading comprehension is an understanding of word meanings and how they connect to other information, ideas, and concepts.

Students with more extensive vocabularies perform better on reading comprehension tasks (NRP, 2000). Vocabulary can be receptive (as in listening, reading) or expressive (speaking, writing). The most effective vocabulary instruction incorporates all four levels of communication. Vocabulary-building methods should provide direct instruction of relevant words, their meanings, and how they are used in context. Additionally, vocabulary instruction should provide strategies for figuring out new words read in context.

Alber and Foil (2003) recommend the following procedure for introducing new vocabulary: (a) present the word by showing it to the students, pronouncing it, and having the students repeat it; (b) provide the definition and many examples of the word used in context; (c) connect the word to students' background knowledge by discussing their related experiences with the word; and (d) provide students with opportunities to use the word in context (make up sentences using the word, read passages containing the word, use new words in written expression). Teachers can also use attention getters to introduce vocabulary. For example, the teacher can wear a silly hat, make up a sentence about it ("I decided to wear an *inane* hat today.") and have students try to figure out the meaning of the word. Teachers can introduce vocabulary by showing pictures or videos, reading interesting sentences or poems, or using props and skits. To promote generalization, teachers should provide positive reinforcement when students use new vocabulary in speaking and writing throughout the day, and recognize newly learned vocabulary when they see or hear it used outside of class. Vocabulary selected for instruction should be based on reading assignments for language arts and content-area texts. The following types of activities can be used to enhance vocabulary development.

Active student responding. Give students several preprinted vocabulary word cards and have them hold up the correct card when they hear the definition or have students write the vocabulary word on dry-erase boards (using a word bank). Students can also work in peer-tutoring dyads to practice defining words or matching words to their definitions. Guided notes can also be helpful to students. For each word, students can write the definition, write examples and nonexamples, draw a picture, and write a sentence using the word. The guided notes can then be used as a study guide for vocabulary tests.

Drama. Using drama for vocabulary instruction is a multisensory approach that includes physical actions to enhance learning. Alber and Foil (2003) suggest the following drama activities:

- *Individual pantomimes.* Write vocabulary words on small pieces of paper and place them in a hat. Have students reach in the hat and select one piece of paper. After reading the word, have the students pantomime the meaning of the word. For example, if the student selects the word *melancholy,* he might pantomime that word by making a sad facial expression and sighing heavily. The rest of the students try to guess the word from a word bank.
- *Whole-class pantomimes.* Directly teach pantomimes for vocabulary words and have students stand up and simultaneously act

out vocabulary definitions. Alber and Foil (2003) provide the example of *rotation* and *revolution* in the context of earth and space science. When the teacher says the word *rotation,* the students spin around. When she says *revolution,* the students walk around their desks. Students can also pantomime facial expressions of emotion words (such as lugubrious, jovial, astounded, exasperated).

- *Skits.* Teams of students are given a set of vocabulary words. They are challenged to create a brief skit using those words. Allow teams about five minutes to create their skits. After each performance, the teacher leads a discussion of how each team depicted the vocabulary words in context.

Semantic mapping. Semantic mapping is an excellent way to show students how words and concepts are connected. Teachers can use chart paper or an overhead projector to model semantic mapping. Then students can work in groups or individually to create their own semantic maps. For example, the teacher can write the vocabulary word in the middle of the chart ("amphibian"), and have the students respond to three questions that branch out from the word: What is it? (a category of vertebrates), What is it like? (cold blooded, has lungs and gills, lays eggs), What are some examples? (frogs, toads, salamanders). Figure 3.2 shows examples of different types of semantic maps for teaching vocabulary concepts.

List-group-label (Taba, 1967). This vocabulary-building activity helps students categorize words. The teacher writes a category word on the board (for instance, musical instruments), prompts students to generate a list of words that belong to the category (such as drum, xylophone, violin, trumpet, harmonica, cello, flute, piano), and writes them on the board. After creating the list, the students can work in groups to create and label subcategories (like percussion, strings, brass, woodwinds).

Semantic feature analysis (Anders & Bos, 1986). Another way to build vocabulary and categorize concepts is using semantic feature analysis. Figure 3.3 shows an example of a semantic feature analysis matrix. The teachers and students generate a list of related vocabulary words that are written in the left column. At the top of the chart, defining features of the related vocabulary are listed. For each vocabulary word on the list, the students indicate which features apply and which features do not. Students can work together in small groups to create their own semantic feature analysis charts for any content area. These charts can then be used as a study guide or reference tool.

A Tier 1 evidence-based commercial program that improves reading achievement as well as English language development for ELL students is the *Vocabulary Improvement Program for English Language Learners and Their Classmates (VIP).* Using targeted words from weekly reading assignments, the program uses the following sequence: ELL students are given the weekly reading assignment in their native language to preview it before they see it in English. In addition to whole-class instruction, students work in small, heterogeneous groups on vocabulary skills including word associations, synonyms and antonyms, and semantic feature analysis.

Figure 3.2 Examples of Semantic Maps

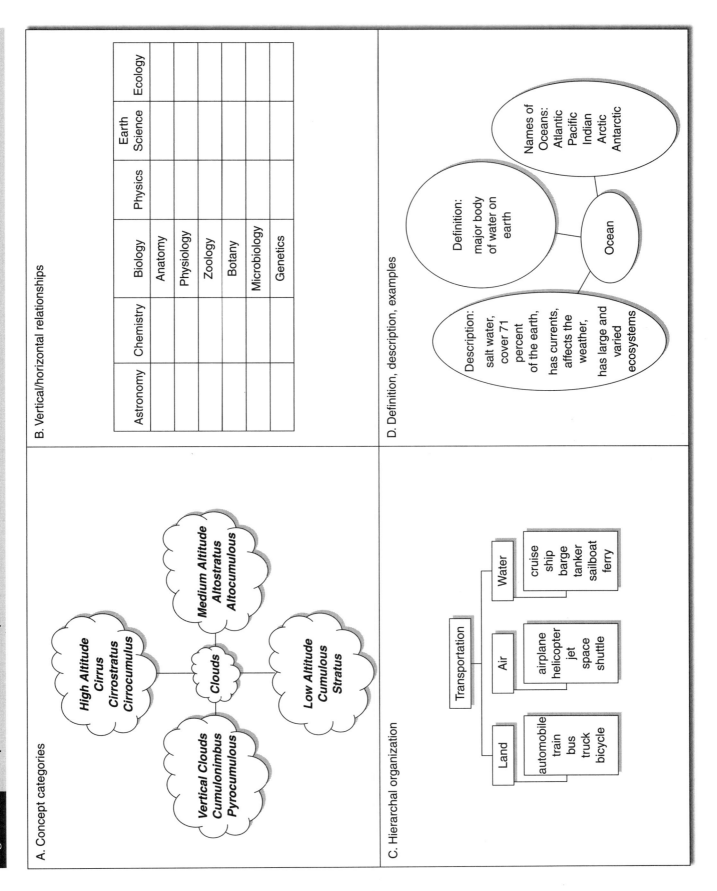

A. Concept categories

B. Vertical/horizontal relationships

C. Hierarchal organization

D. Definition, description, examples

Figure 3.3 Example of a Semantic Feature Analysis Matrix

Features Vertebrates	Warm Blooded	Cold Blooded	Lays Eggs	Live Birth	Produces Milk	Has Lungs	Has Gills	Has Hair	Has Sweat Glands	Has Scales	Has Feathers
Mammals	x			x	x	x		x	x		
Reptiles		x	x			x				x	
Amphibians		x	x			x	x				
Birds	x		x			x					x
Fish		x	x				x			x	

VOCABULARY: TIERS 2 AND 3

For instruction in Tiers 2 and 3, teachers can provide more support with vocabulary development by providing additional practice with using words correctly in context in speaking and writing, figuring out the meaning of words in context, creating semantic maps, and categorizing words. Students can practice vocabulary by sorting words into categories or generating synonyms and antonyms for vocabulary words. As students learn more vocabulary words, teachers can increase the number of words to be categorized into either self-selected or teacher-selected categories.

Students can also preview assigned reading passages and highlight all of the words they do not know. These words can be selected for direct instruction, word sorting, semantic mapping, and active student responding activities. For reference during reading and writing, students can also keep a personalized list of new vocabulary words and their definitions in their notebooks. Students can also keep a box of index cards showing the vocabulary word on one side and the definition and a picture on the other side. They can study their individualized sets of vocabulary words independently, with a peer, or with a teacher.

Another way to help students study is by teaching them to use mnemonic strategies to remember vocabulary words and their definitions (Mastropieri & Scruggs, 1998). The Keyword Method (Atkinson, 1975) is a strategy for making an unfamiliar word more memorable by creating a concrete image. For example, a student might recall that *apex* means high point by thinking of an *ape* at the top of a mountain (Mastropieri, Scruggs, & Fulk, 1990). A student might recall that *antique* means very old by thinking of his elderly *aunt,* or might remember that *ebullient* means happy by thinking of a happy bull (Leaf, 1936). The three-step process for using the Keyword Method is recoding, relating, and retrieving (Levin, 1988). *Recoding* means that the student changes the new vocabulary word to a similar-sounding word that is familiar. *Relating* requires the student to draw a picture of the keyword image illustrating the meaning of the vocabulary word. *Retrieving* requires the student to think of the keyword and image together in order to state the definition. When presented with the word *buoyant,* a student might picture a *boy* floating on a raft, and state that *buoyant* means *floating.* When presented with the word *fetid,* a student might picture stinky feet to remember that fetid means *foul odor* (Foil & Alber, 2002).

IT FITS (King-Sears, Mercer, & Sindelar, 1992) is a strategy for creating and using keywords to learn vocabulary definitions. The steps are: (1) **I**dentify the vocabulary word (for example, nexus), (2) **T**ell the definition (connection or link), (3) **F**ind a keyword (connects us), (4) **I**magine the definition doing something with the keyword (a line of stick-figure people holding hands to make themselves connected), (5) **T**hink about the definition as it relates to the keyword, and (6) **S**tudy the word and image until you can define the word.

COMPREHENSION: TIER 1

Reading comprehension—the whole purpose of reading—requires a synthesis of the above skills, along with sufficient background knowledge and self-regulation strategies (that is, monitoring comprehension while reading).

Students with good reading comprehension skills are able to identify the main idea, sequence information, identify cause-effect relationships, and make predictions. The National Reading Panel (2000) identified the following evidence-based strategies for teaching reading comprehension: answering questions, monitoring comprehension through self-questioning, completing graphic organizers, examining text structure, summarizing, and learning in cooperative groups. These strategies are all used in the following Tier 1 instructional activities.

Answering questions. Students should answer questions before, during, and after reading and receive continuous feedback. Prior to having students read a specific passage, teachers should motivate student interest by leading a discussion about why the topic is personally relevant. Stimulate background knowledge by asking students what they already know about the selected reading topic and what experiences they have had related to the topic. Teachers can also build additional background knowledge using discussion, pictures, videos, demonstrations, or literature. Before reading, students should be directed to preview the text by looking at the title and first sentences, headings, and illustrations. Then teachers ask students what they think they will learn from the story and what predictions they have about the story.

During guided reading, ask students questions that will keep them focused on the important ideas. Stop at specific points in the text and ask students to make inferences, identify cause-effect relationships, or summarize the main points. Periodically ask students to confirm or refute their predictions and make further predictions. Use a "think/pair/share" approach to keep students actively involved with the reading passage and increase their likelihood of success. For this activity, the teacher asks a question, each pair of students briefly discuss the answer, and individual students volunteer to answer in front of the class. After the students finish reading, they can work in pairs or groups to answer written questions, confirm or refute final predictions, retell the story, make up alternate endings, summarize main ideas, or write a reaction.

Monitoring comprehension. Students can use self-questioning strategies to monitor their comprehension while reading. Teachers can provide students with a few generic questions that match the type of text structure of the reading passage. For example, a narrative fiction text may include the following questions: Who is the story about? Where does the story take place? What is the problem? How does the problem get resolved? How did the story end? An expository passage may include generic questions like the following: What is the main idea of this paragraph? What are the supporting details? What does the author want me to learn? Students can stop periodically throughout the passage and ask themselves these questions to monitor their comprehension. If they do not know the answer, they should go back and reread the section to see if they can figure it out. After students have practiced using generic questions they should be encouraged to make up their own questions to monitor comprehension during reading. Teaching students to identify the text structure prior to reading will help them decide which questions to ask.

Completing graphic organizers. Before, during, and after reading, students can complete graphic organizers to enhance their reading comprehension and help them learn different text structures. Knowledge of text structures will help students organize and recall content. Figure 3.4

Figure 3.4	Graphic Organizer for Narrative Reading Passages

Title: Anansi the Spider   **Author: Gerald McDermott**

> **Characters: Anansi, his six sons, and Nyame**
>
> **Setting: The African wilderness**

Problem:

> **Anansi went a long way from home and got lost.**

Events:

1	2	3	4
His sons rescued him from a fish who was trying to eat him.	His sons rescued him from a bird who was trying to eat him.	On the way home, they saw a globe of light in the forest.	Anansi asked Nyame (the god of all things) to help him decide which son deserved to have the globe of light.

Ending:

> **Since all of the sons deserved the prize, Nyame put it in the sky so everyone can see it. It's the moon.**

shows an example of a graphic organizer students can use for narrative reading passages. For expository reading passages, students can use graphic organizers like the one illustrated in Figure 3.5. Teachers should provide direct instruction and guided practice for completing graphic organizers prior to having students work independently.

Summarizing. Summarizing has been demonstrated to be an evidence-based practice for increasing both reading and writing skills (Graham & Perin, 2007). Students can learn to summarize using a strategy called *paragraph shrinking* (McMaster, Fuchs, & Fuchs, 2006). After reading each paragraph in a reading passage, the student stops, identifies the main idea and two details, and states a paragraph summary in 10 words or less. Students can do this exercise independently or with a peer. Students can also stop after reading each section of a passage and write a complete sentence that captures the main idea of that section. At the end of the passage, students can use the main idea sentences to write a summary of the whole reading selection.

Figure 3.5 Example of a Main-Idea Map for an Expository Reading Selection

Theme: Rocks

Paragraph 1

Main Idea: Rocks are classified in different ways.

Details
- Rocks are classified by composition, texture, and size of particles, and how they were formed.
- Three classifications: igneous, sedimentary, metamorphic

Paragraph 2   *Paragraph 3*   *Paragraph 4*

Main Idea: Igneous rocks are formed when molten magma cools.	**Main Idea:** Sedimentary rocks are formed near the earth's surface.	**Main Idea:** Metamorphic rocks are formed by heat and pressure.

Details
 • Plutonic igneous rocks come from the earth's crust.
   ○ Example: granite
 • Volcanic igneous rocks come from volcano lava.
   ○ Example: pumice, obsidian
	Details
	 • Formed by compacting mineral deposits
	   ○ Examples: shale, sandstone, limestone obsidian
		Details
		 • Temperature must be hot enough to make minerals change into different forms.
		   ○ Examples: marble, slate, quartzite

Paragraph 5

Main Idea: Big impact on human advancement

Details
- Used as tools for more than 2 million years
- Human technology progressed at different rates because of metals/rocks present in different regions.

Another reading comprehension strategy that uses summarizing is SQ3R (Robinson, 1970), which uses the following steps: (1) *Survey* (examine title, self-question knowledge of topic, preview text, read the first paragraph, read the last paragraph), (2) *Question* (change the title to a question; change headings, subheadings, and illustrations into questions, write down unknown vocabulary words and find out what they mean), (3) *Read Actively* (find answers to questions generated in Step 2, use context clues to decode unknown words, generate additional questions about anything that is unclear), (4) *Recite* (recall what was read without looking at the answers, recite the answers, and reread parts of the passage if any questions are unanswered), and (5) *Review* (examine answers and organize the information, write a summary of the information, create a graphic organizer, and participate in a group discussion).

Cooperative learning. For each of the above activities students can work with a peer buddy or a cooperative learning group. Students can practice comprehension strategies (such as summarizing, or SQ3R) by working together to apply the strategy and helping each other work through difficult questions. *Literature Circles* (Anderson & Corbet, 2008) is a cooperative learning activity that provides students with opportunities for in-depth discussion of the text. Small heterogeneous groups of students reflect on the reading passage, share their reactions to the story, and listen to each other's opinions. A list of teacher-made questions can be used to guide the discussion during *literature circles.* Another kind of cooperative learning arrangement is called *Jigsaw* (Aronson, Blaney, Stephin, Sikes, & Snapp, 1978). In this arrangement, each group member is assigned to be an "expert" on one section of the text. After each student reads and studies his or her part, the students take turns teaching their respective sections to the rest of the group and answering their questions.

COMPREHENSION: TIERS 2 AND 3

Students needing more intensive instruction in reading comprehension benefit a great deal from small-group and one-on-one instruction because they have more opportunities to make in-depth responses and receive immediate and specific feedback.

Answering questions. As often as possible, teachers should incorporate small-group discussion of reading assignments for struggling readers. Small group instruction allows students to answer more questions, elaborate on their responses, and practice more spoken language. This is especially helpful for ELL students. During small-group discussion, teachers should encourage critical thinking and language development by asking literal and inferential questions, asking follow-up questions for clarification, and prompting students to elaborate on their responses. Teachers should also model expansion and elaboration by repeating student responses back with more detail.

Monitoring comprehension. Students receiving instruction in Tiers 2 or 3 can monitor their comprehension through self-questioning using structured worksheets. With structured worksheets, students read a text that has several predetermined stopping points the teacher has marked in the text. At each stopping point, the student stops reading and answers a series of questions listed on the structured worksheet. Structured worksheets have been demonstrated to increase reading comprehension of middle and high school students (Alber, Nelson, & Brennan, 2002). Instead of writing their answers on structured worksheets, students with severe writing difficulties can also tape-record their responses at each stopping point and review them at the end (Taylor, Alber, & Walker, 2002).

Students can also monitor their reading comprehension using the *Click or Clunk* technique (Wright, 2001). At the end of each sentence, the student self-questions, "Did I understand that?" If the answer is *yes*, the student says "click" and continues reading. If the answer is *no*, the student says "clunk" and rereads the sentence and the next sentence. If it is still a "clunk," the student can reread the paragraph, and if that does not work, he can ask for help.

Completing graphic organizers. Students receiving instruction in Tiers 2 and 3 can be guided through developing their own graphic organizers after the teacher provides a demonstration for the whole class. For example, teachers can provide small-group or one-on-one instruction for creating a narrative story map. Teachers can read a story aloud and guide the students through identifying the main characters, setting, problem, and so on. After students can demonstrate proficiency during guided practice, they can practice more independently.

A simple graphic organizer for helping students with expository writing is a K-W-L chart. This can be used with the whole class, small groups, or individual students. The student folds a piece of paper into thirds to form three vertical columns and writes K at the top of the first column, W at the top of the second column, and L at the top of the third column. The teacher introduces the student to a reading passage about specific content (for instance, whales). Under K (what I *know*), the student generates a list of phrases indicating what he already knows about the topic (whales eat plankton, whales are mammals, whales are the biggest animals). Under W (What I *want* to know), the student generates a list of questions about the topic (How long do whales live? How much do whales weigh? What kind of whale is the biggest?). After reading the passage, the student answers the questions he generated in the W column by completing the column under L (What I *learned*).

The following are examples of Tiers 2 and 3 reading programs demonstrated to be evidence-based for increasing comprehension. *Kaplan SpellRead,* is a K–12 program in which students receive small-group instruction during 60–90 minute blocks. Each lesson includes activities for developing basic reading and fluency skills as well as reading comprehension skills. *Instructional Conversations and Literature Logs* is an evidence-based program for ELL students. Examples of reading comprehension exercises include writing and discussing personal experiences related to characters in a story, descriptions of story events, or evaluations of the story.

SUMMARY

Reading is a critical skill for independent and successful functioning throughout life. Unfortunately, far too many children struggle to read proficiently. In order to address this problem, recent legislation (NCLB, 2002; IDEIA, 2004) has increased teacher accountability for student outcomes in reading and requires teachers to use evidence-based practices to make instructional decisions. IDEIA permits teachers to use a Response to Intervention (RTI) model to identify students with learning disabilities. However, RTI models have been demonstrated to be highly effective for designing reading instruction for all students in inclusive classrooms. Using a three-tiered RTI model, teachers can effectively differentiate reading instruction and apply appropriate levels of intensity as needed by individual students.

Proficient readers must be able to integrate phonemic awareness, alphabetic principle (phonics), fluency, vocabulary, and comprehension. A balanced reading program incorporates all of these skills into daily reading instruction. Teachers can use numerous motivational whole-class, small-group, and individual activities to teach each of the five component reading skills. Evidence-based Tier 1 reading interventions include reading activities such as direct instruction, choral responding, response cards, guided notes, and peer-mediated instruction. Reading instruction in Tiers 2 and 3 may include supplemental practice, multisensory activities, or direct instruction of learning strategies. Teachers can also use commercial programs such as *Peer Assisted Learning Strategies* or *SRA Reading Mastery* to provide Tier 1 reading instruction and *Corrective Reading* or *Wilson Reading System* for instruction in Tiers 2 and 3 (see Table 3.1). To be most effective, reading instruction must provide students with explicit instruction, frequent practice with immediate and specific feedback, and frequent opportunities to apply their reading skills to a variety of authentic contexts.

ALEXEI

Alexei held his blue marker positioned to write the next word on his dry-erase board. He listened carefully when Ms. Olivet asked the next question. "What word means 'to make an already bad situation worse'?" Alexei looked at the word choices written on the board. He recognized the correct answer, "exacerbate," because he remembered it from the story he practiced over the weekend. Since English is Alexei's second language (he was adopted from an orphanage in Russia last summer), Ms. Olivet always lets him take the story and vocabulary words home to practice with his parents before she introduces the story on Mondays. Alexei copied the word "exacerbate" onto his dry-erase board, looked at Brian's board to see if he wrote the same answer (he did), and waited for his teacher to say, "Boards up!"

"Very good, the correct word is 'exacerbate.'" After Ms. Olivet finished reviewing the vocabulary words with the whole class, she directed the students to take out their classwide peer tutoring folders and stories. Alexei always enjoyed taking turns reading with a partner and giving feedback. He was happy to be paired with Brian this week. Brian read first. For each sentence Brian read correctly, Alexei wrote slash marks through two numbers on the point sheet. When it was Alexei's turn to read, he only made a few mistakes. For each mistake, Brian said, "Stop, that word is . . .". Then Alexei reread the sentence correctly and earned one point for that sentence. After they each read the story they took turns asking each other the "who, what, where, when, and why" questions about the story.

Both Ms. Tate and Ms. Olivet walked around the room and gave extra points while saying things like, "Good job giving feedback," and "I like how you're paying attention." They also helped if neither reading partner could figure out a word. After classwide peer tutoring, Alexei and four other students went to work at the listening center where they put on headphones and listened to a story of their choice. One group of students worked with Ms. Olivet, another group of students worked with Ms. Tate, and the rest of the students worked either at the reading center or the computers.

4

Assessing for Intervention in Writing

RTI AND WRITING ASSESSMENT

As with reading, teachers need efficient, accurate, and sensitive measures to monitor student writing progress so they can plan appropriate multi-tiered instruction within the RTI model. Meaningful assessment of written expression is critical for planning effective instruction. Effective assessment enables teachers to identify the strengths and needs of each student and use that information to make appropriate and timely instructional decisions. Writing assessment can be particularly challenging because good writing is a complex synthesis of many skills. Communicating ideas through written expression first requires some proficiency with writing conventions such as spelling, capitalization, punctuation, word usage, and sentence construction. Effective writers must also be able to organize, develop, and support their ideas, express their ideas in a focused and coherent manner; and accurately self-evaluate their writing for revising and editing purposes. More advanced writers are also able to captivate their audience with a strong voice and unique perspective.

Considering the complexity of writing development and the span of student capabilities in inclusive classrooms, writing assessment can become difficult to manage. Fortunately, empirical research provides teachers with efficient methods for assessing written expression and monitoring progress over time. These assessments can provide teachers with meaningful information for planning differentiated instruction that will help all students produce more sophisticated writing. As with reading, curriculum-based measures of writing provide a relatively quick and reliable way to monitor overall writing performance. Using CBM writing, teachers can graph student performance to determine the extent to which students are responding to intervention and identify the students who need more intensive writing instruction. Rubrics can supplement information from CBM writing and help teachers target specific areas of need. This chapter presents the following practical strategies for assessing written expression: curriculum-based measurement, rubrics, and portfolios.

CBM WRITING MEASURES

Research demonstrates that CBM writing measures are valid and reliable predictors of overall writing quality for diverse learners with and without disabilities across grade levels (Espin, De La Paz, Scierka, & Roelofs, 2005; Espin et al., 2008). CBM writing is beneficial in inclusive classrooms because it provides teachers with a quick and easy way to assess and monitor writing performance for instructional planning. Specifically, the teacher obtains a three-minute writing sample and evaluates the sample for the following quantitative elements that are correlated with overall writing quality: total words written (TWW), words spelled correctly (WSC), and correct word sequences (CWS).

After the student completes the three-minute writing sample, the teacher counts the total number of words written and the total number of words spelled correctly. A word is defined as "any series of letters separated from another series of letters by a space" (Espin et al., 2000, p. 144). The teacher will also score the number of correct word sequences in the writing sample. Correct word sequences are pairs of adjacent words that are spelled correctly and used correctly in context (Videen, Deno, & Marston, 1982). To determine the number of correct word sequences, each adjacent pair of words is marked as correct (^) or incorrect (‾) and then counted. Correct capitalization and punctuation are also counted when calculating correct word sequences. For example, the following sentence contains four CWS:

^I ^ like ^ to—colect—basball—cards^.

For secondary students, total words written, words spelled correctly, and correct word sequences are all valid indicators of writing performance. However, research demonstrates that correct word sequences minus incorrect word sequences (CIWS) is the most valid and reliable growth indicator of writing proficiency for middle school students (Espin et al., 2000, 2005) and high school students (Espin et al., 2008). The procedure for calculating CIWS is counting the total number of correct word sequences (CWS) and subtracting the total number of incorrect word sequences (IWS). In the same example above, there are four correct word sequences and three incorrect word sequences, so there is one CIWS (4 CWS—3 IWS = 1 CIWS).

In addition to monitoring CIWS, middle and high school teachers may consider using additional CBM measures to obtain a more accurate evaluation of written expression. Espin, Scierka, Skare, and Halverson (1999) found that combining several CBM measures best predicts the writing performance of secondary students. Specifically, a combination of the following three measures resulted in more accurate predictions of writing ability: number of characters per word, number of sentences, and mean length of correct word sequences.

Because calculating characters per word can be very inefficient and time consuming, teachers should only use this measure if the students type their stories onto a word processing program. Once the story is typed, select the story and click on "word count." A statistics box will appear on the computer screen that shows, among other data, the number of words written and the number of characters. To obtain the number of characters per word, divide the total number of letters by the total number of words (letters/words). Espin and colleagues (1999) calculated the number of sentences by counting each string of words separated from another string by end punctuation (period, question mark, or exclamation point). Mean length of CWS was calculated by counting the number of CWS strings (consecutively occurring CWS) and dividing the total number of CWS by the number of CWS strings.

MANAGING CBM WRITING

The following section describes procedures for implementing CBM for written expression: administering CBM writing, scoring writing samples, graphing data, and making instructional decisions.

Administering CBM writing. Before assessing written expression, teachers must first obtain a brief writing sample in which the students write for three minutes in response to a story starter. Story starters are brief sentences designed to stimulate student writing, such as:

- When I got to school, I was surprised to see . . .
- My best friend and I like to . . .

Story starters should be age appropriate and consistent in difficulty level. They should also have a theme that is familiar to students in order to stimulate their background knowledge (Hosp, Hosp, & Howell, 2007). Teachers can develop their own story starters or use commercially available story starters. For example, AIMSweb provides an extensive list of story starters for each grade and ability level.

After selecting a story starter, the teacher provides the students with lined paper with the story starter printed on top. Teachers may also write the story starter on the chalkboard, overhead projector, or large chart paper. Powell-Smith and Shinn (2004) recommend the following procedures for administering CBM writing:

1. Direct students to write their names at the top of their papers and read the standardized administration directions aloud. For example, "You are going to write a story. First, I will read a sentence, and then you will write a story about what happens next" (Powell-Smith & Shinn, 2004, p. 8). Tell the students how long they have to think about the topic before they begin writing (for example, one minute) and the amount of time they have to write (three minutes).

2. Give students one minute to think about what they are going to write. After 30 seconds, remind the students they should be thinking about the specific story-starter topic. For example, "You should be thinking about . . ." (Powell-Smith & Shinn, 2004, p. 8).

3. After the one-minute thinking time, tell students to begin writing. After 90 seconds of writing, remind the students of what they should be writing about.

4. After three minutes of writing, tell the students to stop and put their pencils down.

Students should be allowed to finish writing their stories after the time limit if they want to, but they should finish on another piece of paper or mark the place where they were told to stop. Then the teacher will be able to score only the writing that occurred during the three minutes.

According to Powell-Smith and Shinn (2004), the above administration procedures are most appropriate for elementary students and students with writing difficulties. However, secondary students should be provided with more time to write because that will produce a more accurate measure of writing quality (Espin et al., 2008). Fuchs and Fuchs (2007) recommend three-minute writing samples for middle elementary students, five-minute writing samples for late elementary students, and seven-minute writing samples for middle and high school students. Additionally, Fuchs and Fuchs recommend giving students 30 seconds to think about their writing instead of one minute. After teachers select the most appropriate CBM procedures for their students (such as time limits, prompts) they should be sure to administer the CBM the same way every time. This will provide for a more accurate comparison of current performance to previous performance. For students who struggle with writing, teachers should administer CBM writing probes once or twice each week depending on the severity of the writing problems. High-performing students only need to be assessed every few weeks or monthly (Hosp et al., 2007).

Score writing samples. When planning for CBM writing, teachers should decide which measures are most appropriate for their students and most feasible to implement. Teachers can use the same writing samples to calculate total words written (TWW), words spelled correctly (WSC), correct word sequences (CWS), and correct word sequences minus incorrect word sequences (CIWS).

Graphing data. In order to graph CBM data, the teacher will need to use graph paper or a computer program (such as Excel) to create a line graph that shows the rate of student progress over time. Excel templates for graphing CBM data are available at Progressmonitoring.com. Additionally, graphing programs are available at the following CBM Web sites: Edcheckup (www.edcheckup.com), AIMSweb (www.aimsweb.com), and Intervention Central (www.interventioncentral.org).

After selecting a mode for graphing student data, start by creating a vertical axis and a horizontal axis (see Figure 4.1). The vertical axis will show the student's CBM scores (such as Correct Word Sequences) and the horizontal axis will show when the student attained those scores (Week 1, Week 2, and so on). The horizontal axis should show each week until the end of the school year. Examining the data path will help teachers

| Figure 4.1 | Fremont's CBM Writing Data (Correct Word Sequences) |

determine the effectiveness of an intervention and whether or not they need to modify instruction. Figure 4.1 shows an example of a line graph used for monitoring the writing progress of a fourth grader with writing difficulties (Fremont). Teachers may use the following steps for monitoring student progress.

1. *Collect and graph baseline data.* To collect baseline data, administer a series of at least three CBM writing probes before any intervention is implemented. Baseline data provides information about the student's present levels of performance and enables the teacher to set appropriate goals. Hosp and colleagues (2007) recommend teachers administer the three baseline data probes on the same day or on three consecutive days. Figure 4.1 shows that Fremont scored 13, 17, and 16 correct word sequences during three consecutive days.

2. *Set appropriate goals.* After plotting the baseline data, determine the median score. The median score falls between the highest and lowest score. Fremont's median score is 16. In order to set appropriate goals, the teacher should look at the norm table for CBM writing available on AIMSweb. The norm table shows that a fourth grader scoring 16 CWS on a writing probe in the fall is performing at the twenty-fifth percentile. To set an appropriately ambitious goal, the teacher should look at the norm table to find out the mean CBM of average-performing students in spring quarter. For lower-performing students, the goal should be to perform in the average range (that is, the fiftieth percentile) compared to same-grade-level peers. For higher-performing students, appropriate goals might be performance in the seventy-fifth percentile. The norm table shows that a fourth grader who scores 39 CWS during spring quarter is performing at the

fiftieth percentile. If Fremont attains 39 CWS by spring, he will be performing in the average range for a fourth grader. So, Fremont's teacher decides that 39 CWS is an appropriate goal for Fremont.

3. *Draw an aim line.* The aim line is the line that connects the median baseline data point to the goal. Before any intervention data are collected, Fremont's teacher draws a line from his median baseline data point (16 CWS) to his goal (39 CWS). The line will enable the teacher to determine if Fremont is progressing at the expected rate toward his goal. If Fremont is progressing on target, all of the remaining CWS data points will be close to the aim line.

4. *Continue collecting and graphing CBM data regularly.* First, draw a phase-change line that shows when the intervention is implemented, and continue collecting data as frequently as necessary. Based on Fremont's performance during baseline testing and the feasibility of classroom demands, the teacher decides to collect CBM data for Fremont on a weekly basis.

5. *Use the data to make instructional decisions.* In order to enhance the effectiveness of CBM, teachers must consistently employ decision rules when examining student data. The same three-data-point rule used in CBM reading is also used in CBM writing. If the data points are clustered close to the aim line, above and below, no change of instruction is needed because the student is progressing at the expected rate. If three consecutive data points are above the aim line, the end goal should be raised to reflect a more ambitious rate of progress. If three consecutive data points fall below the aim line, instruction should be modified.

6. *Modifying instruction.* When modifying instruction, draw a phase-change line and label the new phase. Figure 4.1 shows that during Intervention 1, Fremont's data fell below the aim line on three consecutive sessions. So, his teacher decided to modify instruction. She noticed that Fremont was frequently off task during writing practice, so she taught him to use a self-monitoring system and reinforced him for writing a predetermined number of words during each writing session. After implementing self-monitoring and reinforcement, the number of Fremont's CWS increased to the expected rate when compared to his aim line.

CBM writing is efficient for collecting information about overall writing proficiency because it can be administered to the whole class at the same time in about five minutes. Teachers should administer CBM writing probes to all students at least three times each school year (fall, winter, spring) for screening and benchmarking purposes (Hosp et al., 2007). Based on the results of screening, teachers can determine the frequency with which to monitor student progress using CBM writing.

Teachers can organize CBM materials by creating a folder for each student that contains their CBM writing samples, scoring sheets, and graphs. The files can be color coded by frequency of scheduled probes. General and special education teachers can collaborate to organize, administer, score, graph, and analyze CBM writing for all students in the inclusive classroom. Throughout the school year, teachers will be able to examine individual CBM probe data to determine if students are making sufficient progress toward their goals. If students are not making sufficient progress, teachers will need to determine specific areas of need in order to plan appropriate instruction.

Although CBM is a valid and reliable indicator of overall writing development, teachers can obtain more specific information by examining the types of errors students make on their three-minute writing probes. For example, teachers can create a form that lists categories of errors such as punctuation, spelling, capitalization, and grammar. While examining a student's writing piece, the teacher can tally the number of each type of error. The results of the error analysis will provide teachers with more direction for which skills to target. The most frequently occurring errors should probably be addressed first. Subsequent error analysis checks will help teachers determine the extent to which their remediation is effective.

Teachers can also create an error-analysis form that provides more specific information about the types of writing errors. For example, Hessler and Konrad (2008) created an error-analysis matrix to help teachers identify the frequency of each type of spelling, punctuation, capitalization, usage, and style error. Under each category of errors, the teacher can create individualized checklists. For example, Hessler and Konrad show a form for a student named Camille. Under the category of spelling, some of the types of errors listed on Camille's matrix were blend and diagraph errors, reversals, and schwa errors. Under the category of punctuation, the types of errors listed for Camille included end punctuation, different types of comma errors, and quotation marks. The error-analysis matrix is flexible and can be adjusted for the curriculum requirements at each grade level. It can also be modified for individual students based on their writing needs. After tallying errors for each student, teachers can plan whole-class, small-group, or individual instruction based on the number of students making the same types of writing errors (Hessler & Konrad, 2008).

WRITING RUBRICS

Another useful tool for writing assessment is a rubric. Writing rubrics can help teachers determine levels of writing proficiency and quality by comparing student performance to predetermined criteria (Mueller, 2008). Rubrics can be general and apply to a wide range of writing tasks, or they can be specific to one type of writing (such as narrative or persuasive). Depending on the purpose of the assessment, teachers can use holistic or analytical rubrics to assess writing. Holistic rubrics are used to quickly score a writing piece based on its overall impression. For example, Fairfax County Public Schools (2004) provides a holistic rubric that allows teachers to rate student writing on the combined elements of task completion, comprehensibility, level of discourse, vocabulary, language control, and mechanics. Based on their overall performance, students can receive one of the following scores: 4—Exceeds Expectations, 3—Meets Expectations, 2—Almost Meets Expectations, and 1—Does Not Meet Expectations.

Figure 4.2 shows an example of a holistic rubric for fiction writing.

Figure 4.2	Holistic Rubric for Fiction Writing

4	• Original and interesting ideas • Varied sentence structure • Descriptive sentences • Logical progression of the story (beginning, middle, end) • All essential story elements are included (characters, setting, problem, resolution) • Fairly advanced use of vocabulary • Relatively free of grammar, spelling, capitalization, and punctuation errors
3	• Some interesting ideas and details • Sentences are complete and show some variation of structure • Most ideas are in sequential order • At least three essential story elements are included (characters, setting, problem, resolution) • Average to above-average use of vocabulary • Few grammar, spelling, capitalization, and/or punctuation errors
2	• Ideas show limited originality • Most sentences are complete, but lack structural variation • Some sentences are incomplete or incoherent • Less than three essential story elements are present • Immature use of vocabulary • Frequent grammar, spelling, capitalization, and/or punctuation errors
1	• Ideas are unclear • Most sentences are incomplete or incoherent • No logical sequence of ideas • Inaccurate and immature use of vocabulary • Almost all sentences have grammar, spelling, capitalization, and/or punctuation errors

Teachers can develop and customize rubrics for different types of writing and emphasize different important elements. One way to develop a holistic rubric is to obtain a three-minute writing sample from each student. Read through the writing samples quickly and, based on overall impression, place them in four piles ranging from most proficient to least proficient. Then examine the writing samples in each pile to determine the elements in common at each level. Those will be the elements used in the rubric. For example, Figure 4.2 shows a rubric with elements that include originality, sentence structure, description, logical progression of ideas, use of story elements, use of vocabulary, and number of mechanical errors. Another good way for teachers to develop useful rubrics is to locate rubrics that have already been developed and modify them to fit the needs of their students within the writing curriculum. Table 4.1 shows Web sites where teachers can find writing rubrics that are both holistic and analytical.

Table 4.1	Web sites for Obtaining and/or Creating Writing Rubrics

About.com: Secondary Education
http://712educators.about.com/od/rubrics/Rubrics_Writing_and_Grading_Rubrics.htm

Great Source I Write
http://www.greatsource.com/iwrite/educators/e_rubrics.html

Rubistar
http://rubistar.4teachers.org/index.php

Rubrics for Assessment
http://www.uwstout.edu/soe/profdev/rubrics.shtml

Rubrics 4 Teachers
http://www.rubrics4teachers.com/writing.php

Rubrician
http://www.rubrician.com/writing.htm

Teach-nology
http://teach-nology.com/web_tools/rubrics/writing/

Web English Teacher
http://www.webenglishteacher.com/rubrics.html

Writing with Writers
http://teacher.scholastic.com/writewit/tguide/assess_eval.htm

Although it may take more time to score, an analytical rubric may be more useful because it allows the teacher to assess each writing element separately. Analytical rubrics are usually better assessment tools for students with disabilities and English language learners because these students' levels of proficiency within each writing element may be very different (Wiig, 2000). Analytical rubrics provide criteria for assessing student performance on each element of the writing piece. For example, the *6+1 Trait Writing* rubric provides a separate rating scale for each of the following components of a writing piece: ideas, organization, voice, word choice, sentence fluency, conventions, and presentation. Each of those aspects is rated as either: 5—Strong, 4—Effective, 3—Developing, 2—Emerging, or 1—Not Yet. Because each distinct element of writing performance is rated separately, analytical rubrics provide a more accurate picture of specific strengths and weaknesses in the writing products (Mueller, 2008).

An analytical writing rubric is structured so that the writing qualities are identified, a rating scale is determined for each quality, and the characteristics of performance for each quality are described (Schirmer & Bailey, 2000). The writing qualities selected for a rubric will vary across grade and ability levels, but most writing rubrics contain similar categories. In order to create an analytical rubric, teachers must decide which critical elements to assess and how each level of performance will be defined. Teachers should select writing elements that are most useful in the context of their students' ages, ability levels, writing goals of the curriculum, and types of writing tasks. Figure 4.3 shows an example of an analytical writing rubric for persuasive writing.

Figure 4.3 Analytical Rubric for Persuasive Writing

Skill	4	3	2	1
Introduction	First paragraph has an effective attention grabber, clear position statement, and presents main ideas that will be discussed.	First paragraph has an attention grabber that is not very strong, a position statement that needs additional clarity, and includes some of the main ideas that will be discussed.	An attention grabber is attempted but lacks clarity and connection to the position statement. Position statement is vague, and main ideas that will be presented are not included.	No attention grabber, incoherent or nonexistent position statement, and no mention of the main ideas that will be presented
Organization	Essay is presented in logical order with the presentation of arguments in order of most to least important.	Essay presents each argument clearly, but not in the correct sequence.	Essay lacks overall organization. Arguments are presented randomly.	No organization detected, arguments are unclear, reads like free association.
Audience	Clear identification of the intended audience, and appropriate writing style, vocabulary, and arguments for that audience.	Less-clear idea of the audience. Writing style, vocabulary, and arguments are not always consistent with the target audience.	Vague idea of the target audience, some arguments seem to be appropriate.	No apparent target audience can be determined.
Main Ideas and Details	Main ideas are clearly stated and supported by at least three details that are either factual or logical.	Main ideas are stated and supported by less than three details. Some details may not be factual, logical, or supportive of the main idea.	Main ideas are stated, but no supporting details are provided.	Main ideas are unclear.
Sentences	Interesting sentences, strong statements, and advanced sentence variation.	Sentences are complete and show some variation of structure.	Sentences show little or no variation. Some sentences are incomplete or incoherent.	Most sentences are incomplete or incoherent.

Skill	4	3	2	1
Conclusion	Main ideas culminate into a strong, clear statement of the author's viewpoint.	Main ideas are restated in the conclusion.	A conclusion is attempted, but the main ideas are unclear.	No conclusion is provided.
Mechanics	Free of grammar, spelling, capitalization, and/or punctuation errors.	Few grammar, spelling, capitalization, and/or punctuation errors.	Many grammar, spelling, capitalization, and/or punctuation errors.	Almost all sentences have grammar, spelling, capitalization, and/or punctuation errors.

PORTFOLIOS

Curriculum-based measurement and writing rubrics provide teachers with relatively efficient ways to evaluate writing proficiency and quality. CBM also provides quantifiable measures that enable the teacher to monitor progress over the course of the school year. In order to provide a more complete picture of writing achievement, teachers should also consider using portfolios. A writing portfolio is a purposeful collection of work that documents a student's performance and illustrates progress over time (Jochum, Curran, & Reetz, 1998).

Collecting and examining authentic student writing pieces throughout the school year allows teachers to continuously evaluate the development of writing skills. As writing pieces are collected, teachers can use rubrics to evaluate overall quality, particular strengths, and areas where improvement is needed. Teachers can supplement holistic and analytical scoring with brief anecdotal evaluations comparing current writing pieces to previous writing pieces in order to determine qualitative growth. Additionally, writing pieces in the portfolios may be examined to determine critical areas of need. Teachers may use any one or a combination of the following types of portfolios described by Swicegood (1994): showcase, cumulative, and goal based.

- *Showcase portfolio.* A showcase portfolio is a collection of complete and polished writing pieces designed as a display for a student's best work. This collection of writing pieces should showcase a wide range of writing purposes (narrative, persuasive, informative, and so on) in order to provide a more complete evaluation of strengths and needs. When using a showcase portfolio, students should be involved in deciding which writing pieces should be included. This enables them to practice self-evaluation and take pride in themselves as authors.
- *Cumulative portfolio.* The purpose of a cumulative portfolio is to document student progress over time. When using a cumulative portfolio, teachers can examine the extent to which a student's writing performance becomes more sophisticated with each attempt. These types of

portfolios also provide teachers with additional qualitative information for planning instruction or remediation and communicating with parents. Within a cumulative portfolio, teachers may document each stage of the writing process for one writing piece. These portfolio items may include brainstorming notes, graphic organizers, outlines, a series of drafts, and the final product.

- *Goal-based portfolio.* Writing pieces that document mastery of objectives make up the items in a goal-based portfolio. This type of portfolio should be used for each student who has an Individual Education Program (IEP). The teacher should place a checklist of the student's IEP objectives for written expression in the portfolio. As the student demonstrates mastery of each writing skill, a permanent product showing evidence of mastery is placed in the goal-based portfolio (for example, a paragraph punctuated correctly to 95 percent accuracy). Goal-based portfolios clearly connect instruction and authentic assessment, provide teachers with specific information to make instructional decisions, and provide parents with a better understanding of student learning (Jochum et al., 1998).

Using technology to create electronic portfolios may be appropriate for many learners in inclusive classrooms. Electronic portfolios can include written expression with multimedia effects (such as pictures, sounds, animation). This may be very motivating for some students and may help them increase their proficiency with computers. Chapter 5 provides suggestions for helping students use technology to produce written expression.

SUMMARY

Accurate and efficient writing assessment is necessary for providing students with appropriate writing instruction. The complexity of written expression can make progress monitoring difficult and time consuming. CBM writing is a straightforward and efficient way to assess student performance. CBM writing offers several quantifiable measures that provide teachers with continuous data on overall writing performance. These data can be used to make instructional decisions about the intensity of writing instruction needed by each student. Reliable predictors of writing achievement for elementary students include total words written (TWW), words spelled correctly (WSC), and correct word sequences (CWS). For secondary students, correct word sequences minus incorrect word sequences (CIWS) is a more accurate measure. Teachers in middle and high school may also consider measuring the number of characters per word and the number of sentences written, because these measures are also reliable predictors of writing achievement.

In order to obtain a more complete picture of writing-skill development, teachers should supplement CBM with additional assessments that will help pinpoint specific skills to target for instruction. For example, teachers can do an error analysis of a three-minute writing sample and tally the number of mechanical errors according to type (spelling, punctuation, grammar). An error analysis of student writing may reveal recurring error patterns that teachers can remediate during multitiered instruction.

Writing rubrics also provide useful information. Holistic writing rubrics are relatively quick measures that indicate an overall impression of writing quality. Although more time consuming than holistic rubrics, analytical rubrics allow teachers to determine specific strengths and weaknesses of many different aspects of writing. Students should also keep writing portfolios to showcase their best work, document progress toward their goals, and demonstrate evidence of skill mastery.

DYLAN

Dylan had one minute to think about the story starter that was printed at the top of the page. He wasn't allowed to start writing until his teacher said "Start writing." The story starter was, "'Up we go,' said my friend and…" (from AIMSweb). Dylan thought about what goes up: a rollercoaster, an airplane, a rocket ship, a hot air balloon. He watched a program on the Discovery channel about hot air balloons and he thought about floating in that basket over the ocean with his friend. Which friend? Probably Brett because he was Dylan's best friend and was not afraid of heights. Sometimes Brett got him into trouble so…

"Start writing," Ms. Ruiz said, "you have three minutes."

Dylan whispered to himself, "Up we go, said my friend and…" he continued the sentence with

…the hot air balloon floated into the big blue sky while all of the people, buildings, and cars below got smaller and smaller. Seagulls flew past us. One tried to land on the basket of the balloon. I looked at my friend Brett. This whole thing was his idea. "Hey Brett," I said, "how much trouble do you think we'll be in for borrowing this hot air balloon…".

"OK, time is up," Ms. Ruiz said. "Put your pencils down and pass your paper forward." Ms. Ruiz collected the brief CBM writing samples to assess them for correct word sequences. For the students who had been performing below their aim line, Ms. Ruiz examines their writing passages and documents specific errors. Ms. Ruiz works with Mr. Stein to group students for differentiated writing instruction according their most frequent types of errors. Ms. Ruiz also examines writing portfolios to determine the extent to which student writing has been improving over time. For students like Dylan, who are motivated to excel at writing, Ms Ruiz plans to discuss with her grade-level team ways to challenge Dylan's writing ability.

5

Implementing Multitiered Writing Instruction

Writing instruction has a long history of neglect in US education. This neglect is evident in the most recent report of the National Assessment of Educational Progress (NAEP), which reveals that only about 25 percent of fourth, eighth, and twelfth graders scored at the proficient level on the NAEP writing exam (Persky, Daane, & Jin, 2003). Proficient writing is necessary for successful functioning in school and community environments during childhood and throughout adulthood. Writing performance affects graduation, admission into postsecondary programs, employment options, and social opportunities (Graham & Perin, 2007). As students progress through school, they are met with increasing expectations to demonstrate their knowledge through writing. Additionally, the upsurge of computer technology in the twenty-first century has only increased the need to write (e-mail, Web-based instruction). Students who learn to write well have a powerful tool for communicating, studying, learning, creating, and increasing their quality of life. This chapter will present evidence-based practices for teaching written expression to diverse learners in inclusive classrooms using various instructional arrangements within a three-tiered response to intervention (RTI) model.

Considering the range of unique backgrounds that typify inclusive classrooms, writing instruction can provide exciting and enriching learning experiences for all students, including those who struggle. Struggling writers often have difficulty with transcription, organization, and self-regulation.

Their compositions are shorter, less focused, lacking in detail, and contain more irrelevant information and more mechanical errors (Graham & Harris, 2003; Santangelo & Quint, 2008). Struggling writers also have difficulty critically evaluating how well their writing corresponds to their intended purpose, audience, and genre (Santangelo & Quint, 2008).

In classrooms where students produce exceptional writing, teachers establish high expectations as they provide a supportive environment and frequent opportunities to produce many kinds of writing pieces (Graham, Olinghouse, & Harris, 2009). Excellent writing teachers actively involve students by implementing authentic and interesting writing activities, adapting instruction for diverse learning needs, and teaching students writing skills in whole-class, small-group, and individual teaching arrangements (Graham et al.).

EVIDENCE-BASED PRACTICES

Based on their meta-analysis of research in *Writing Next*, Graham and Perin (2007) identified the following elements as evidence-based practices for improving writing achievement: (a) teaching writing strategies for planning, revising, and editing; (b) teaching summary writing; (c) providing opportunities for collaborative writing with peers; (d) setting clear product goals; (e) using the computer to write; (f) teaching students to combine sentences; (g) teaching prewriting strategies; (h) teaching students to use inquiry skills; (i) teaching the writing process; (j) providing good writing models; and (k) writing for content learning. Additionally, teaching transcription skills (handwriting, keyboarding, and spelling) to beginning and struggling writers produces a positive effect on their writing quality (Graham et al., 2009). Throughout this chapter, the above evidence-based practices are presented within multitiered instruction in each of the following categories: handwriting, keyboarding, spelling, writing process, and using technology for writing.

HANDWRITING INSTRUCTION: TIER 1

Before children can express their ideas coherently in written form, they need to have adequate transcription skills. That is, they need to be able produce legible handwriting with correctly spelled words so their ideas can be deciphered by the reader. Teaching transcription skills can be considered Tier 1 instruction in most early elementary classrooms (K–3), with additional Tiers 2 and 3 supports for students who struggle. For older students, depending on the severity of their difficulties, basic handwriting and spelling instruction will often be needed for Tiers 2 and 3 instruction.

The use of computer technology has decreased the need for handwriting skills, but for most students, handwriting is an unavoidable and important functional skill. Handwriting requires proficient eye-hand coordination, fine motor control, and visual-kinesthetic memory. The progression of handwriting development begins with gross motor arm and wrist movements, and moves toward fine motor finger and thumb movements required for controlled handwriting. When facilitating the development of early handwriting competence, teachers should provide activities that promote fine motor skills, hand dominance, and hand strength. Examples of these activities include coloring, tracing, scribbling, drawing, cutting paper, molding clay, and doing finger plays (such as "Five Little Monkeys," "Where is Thumbkin?").

During the elementary school years, children are expected to learn manuscript handwriting and then cursive handwriting. Some educators question the practice of teaching two different handwriting systems. Manuscript is more legible, easier to learn, less demanding of fine motor skills, and resembles print in books (Hagin, 1983). With cursive handwriting, students are less likely to reverse letters or produce spacing errors. Evidence generally supports teaching manuscript first and transitioning to cursive in second or third grade (Schlagel, 2007).

Manuscript writing instruction usually begins in kindergarten. Two common manuscript (and cursive) formats are Zaner-Bloser and D'Nealian. The Zaner-Bloser method is composed of basic strokes of circles and straight lines. The D'Nealian manuscript alphabet is designed to provide an easier transition from manuscript to cursive handwriting. It is composed of strokes that are oval and slanted with added tails or curves similar to cursive writing.

A multisensory approach is effective for teaching beginning handwriting. In this method, the teacher orally leads students through the formation of a letter, describing the strokes as the students write. Tracing letters, using color-cued lined paper, stencils, templates, and margin underlays can provide guidance for handwriting acquisition. Once students become more proficient, teachers should systematically fade out the verbal cues, colored midlines, and letter tracing guides. Cursive handwriting requires more precise and coordinated fine motor movements than manuscript handwriting. Similar to manuscript handwriting, a multisensory approach and fading model is effective.

When writing on paper, students should be seated comfortably with both forearms on the desk, grasping the pencil above the sharpened point with the writing hand and holding the top of the paper with the other hand. The paper should be parallel to the edge of the desk, not slanted. For cursive handwriting, the paper should be tilted at an angle with the top of the page pointing away from the writing hand. Teachers may want to place masking tape on the desk as a guide to the student for correct paper positioning. The following are recommendations for teaching handwriting (Graham, Harris & Fink, 2000):

- Model the letter by writing it on the board and describing how the letter is formed (for instance, lower case *l*: "Start at the top line, pull down straight"; lower case *b:* "Start at the top line, pull down straight, push up, circle forward"). Point out the similarities and differences of the letter to other letters ("The letter *l* and the letter *b* both start off the same way.").
- Sequence guided practice by having the students trace the letter first, copy the letter from a close model (on the page), copy the letter from a distant model (the board), and then write the letter from memory.

As the students practice, they should also verbalize the steps. Written models should also include numbered arrows to show the sequence for forming the letter.

- Manuscript letters should be introduced in order of easiest to most difficult, progressing from letters with straight lines (for example l, i, t) to letters that include circles and curves (such as c, a, b). For cursive handwriting, Hanover (1983) recommends the following teaching sequence for lower-case letters: "e" family (e, l, h, f, b, k); "i" family (i, t, u); "c" family (c, a, d, o, q, g), handle family (b, o, v, w), hump family (n, m, v, y, x), tails tied in back (f, q), tails tied in front (j, g, p, y, z), and "r" and "s."
- As students are learning to write individual letters, they should progress fairly quickly to writing words, phrases, and sentences.

Effective handwriting programs provide explicit instruction, daily practice in short sessions, and application of skills to meaningful writing tasks (Schlagel, 2007). Immediate and specific feedback and praise are critical for effective writing instruction. In order to facilitate self-regulation and independence, students can practice self-evaluating the quality of their handwriting (Vaughn, Bos, & Schumm, 2006). For example, students can examine a row of letters, draw a circle around their best letters, and rewrite their less legible letters.

HANDWRITING INSTRUCTION: TIERS 2 AND 3

Handwriting difficulties are easy for teachers to identify because poor or illegible handwriting is readily apparent upon visual inspection. Teachers must examine and provide feedback on several aspects of handwriting, including position of the hand and paper, letter size, proportion of letters to each other, quality of the pencil lines, regularity and slant of the letters, letter formation and alignment, letter and word spacing, connection of cursive letters, and speed of production.

For students struggling with handwriting, the cover-copy-compare method can help them practice letter formation and self-evaluation. The student looks at a model of a letter or word, covers it with an index card, writes the letter or word from memory, uncovers the model, and compares his or her word to the model. Then the student rewrites any letters that were formed incorrectly. Self-verbalized instructions have been demonstrated to be effective for correct letter formation (Graham, 1983). The teacher models writing the letter while verbalizing instructions ("letter 'g': start at the middle line; go around; retrace down; and go half a line below the bottom line, hook to the left"), the student practices verbalizing and writing in unison with the teacher, and, finally, the student verbalizes and writes the letter independently. To increase handwriting fluency, students can practice timed repeated writing of the same brief passage, attempting to beat their previous score (Reis, 1989). Zaner-Bloser scales for letters per minute (lpm) proficiency are as follows: first grade—25 *lpm*; second grade—30 *lpm*; third grade—38 *lpm*; fourth grade—45 *lpm*; fifth grade—60 *lpm*, and sixth grade—67 *lpm*.

Students can also work with self-correcting materials such as chemical inks and templates. With chemical inks, the student uses a special pen and treated paper to practice handwriting. The ink color changes when students write outside the letter zone. Additionally, students can self-assess by comparing their letters to a template. At the secondary level, teachers can make handwriting instruction more functional for students by allowing them to write notes or letters to friends, write directions to places of interest, write the names and addresses of friends, write captions for photographs, complete a job application, or write a check.

Examples of writing programs for young children and students who struggle with handwriting include *First Strokes, Pencil Pete's Handwriting, Letterland,* and *Handwriting Without Tears.* These programs include motivating graphics and multisensory activities for improving handwriting. For example, *Handwriting Without Tears* uses multisensory play activities and materials such as Wood Pieces, Roll-A-Dough Letters, Stamp and See Screen, music CDs, and a slate chalkboard. Activities include letter stories, imaginary writing, and mystery letter games.

KEYBOARDING INSTRUCTION

Teaching keyboarding skills is a viable alternative for students who struggle with handwriting. When compared to handwriting, producing written expression at the computer is easier, faster, and more legible. Whether or not they struggle with handwriting, all students need to learn keyboarding skills in order to fully participate in our current computer age.

Keyboarding instruction usually begins at third or fourth grade. To teach keyboarding skills, model and provide feedback for correct positioning. Students should sit up straight, feet flat on the floor, fingers curved and aligned with home keys, and eyes looking straight ahead at the monitor. Keyboarding requires memorization of the letter keys and frequent practice. Ways to practice memorizing the keyboard include having students write the corresponding letters on the back of their fingers or make cut-out hand prints with the letters printed on them. Students can practice examining a keyboard and labeling the keys correctly on a work sheet. Frequent practice is the best way to help students become proficient with keyboarding Teachers can make a series of index cards with directions for different typing tasks. Pairs of students can take turns drawing index cards and performing the skill. For example, "type your name as many times as you can in a minute, blindfolded," or "type the words to your favorite song," or "type the following passage in less than three minutes: (select a brief passage from a favorite book or poem)."

There are several motivating computer programs that teach typing using video games with colorful graphics, animation, sound effects, and music. As students become more proficient, they advance to more difficult levels with different, more challenging games. An example of this kind of keyboarding program is *Jumpstart Typing.* This program simulates a series of games (such as skateboarding, snowboarding, mountain climbing) between two teams. Accurate and fast typing helps students progress through athletic events and avoid obstacles. Similarly motivating programs designed to teach typing include *Mario Teaches Typing 2*, *Mavis Beacon Teaches Typing for Kids*, *SpongeBob Squarepants Typing*, *Typing Tutor 7*, and *Kid Keys*.

SPELLING INSTRUCTION: TIER 1

Spelling is an essential skill for producing written expression. When children are proficient spellers, "they are more likely to focus . . . on clarity, logic, and the substance of their writing, not on the orthography of spelling" (Okyere, Heron, & Goddard, 1997, p. 52). Conversely, children who have spelling difficulties may experience frustration and resistance toward writing activities.

Traditional spelling instruction uses a linguistic approach in which words in basal spelling programs are sequenced and grouped according to phonological and morphological aspects of written language production. Words within each list proceed through a series of lessons focusing on sound symbol relationships, word patterns, rhyming patterns, vowel-change patterns, syllabication, dictionary skills, synonyms, and word usage (Heron, Okyere, & Miller, 1991). In a traditional spelling program, students are given a list of 10 to 20 words on Monday, a series of practice activities using the spelling words each day, and a spelling-dictation test on Friday. Weekly activities in basal spelling programs may include completing alphabetization and syllabication exercises, finding words in the dictionary, writing sentences using the spelling words, and completing word finds or crossword puzzles. One problem with basal spelling programs is they may not provide sufficient practice for some students. For this reason, teachers using basal spelling programs should provide frequent and varied opportunities to increase active student responding (ASR). Choral responding, response cards, peer tutoring, and self-correction are evidence-based practices that should be included in Tier 1 spelling instruction.

Choral responding. Teachers can use direct instruction (model, lead, test) with choral responding to teach spelling words during brief daily practice. For example, the teacher says, "My turn—spell *envelope*, e-n-v-e-l-o-p-e, *envelope*. Together—*spell envelope* . . . Your turn—spell *envelope* . . . ." The students chorally spell the word with the teacher and then without the teacher.

Response cards. Choral responding can be combined with response cards for spelling practice. Students can write their spelling words on dry-erase boards upon teacher prompting ("Spell *watch*.") and hold their cards up for feedback when the teacher signals ("Cards up!"). Students should be encouraged to look at each other's cards and help each other. Alternately, students can be provided with preprinted response cards with "yes" and "no" printed on opposite sides of each card. The teacher can show students different words and ask them to hold up their response cards to indicate whether or not a word is spelled correctly.

Peer tutoring. Students can work in pairs and take turns prompting each other to spell words and providing immediate feedback. In this arrangement, students can practice with individualized sets of words to match their skill levels. For each word spelled correctly, the student can earn two points. If a word is spelled incorrectly, the student writes it correctly three times and earns one point (Greenwood et al., 2001). While monitoring peer tutoring, teachers can also award points for following the procedures correctly, staying on task, and providing appropriate feedback and praise.

Self-correction. With self-correction, students learn to spell by comparing their misspelled words to a model and writing the word correctly. Self-correction has been identified as the most critical element contributing to spelling achievement (Okyere et al., 1997). Teachers can dictate a list of words to students and then provide them with an answer key for self-checking. Students draw a star next to each correctly spelled word and rewrite any misspelled words correctly. Self-correction can also be individualized for struggling spellers. The teacher can audiotape individual word lists with prompts to self-correct. Students can wear headphones and work individually to practice spelling and self-correcting each word.

When making decisions about which words to teach, teachers should select words with similar spelling patterns and words most frequently used in students' writing. Graham, Harris, and Loynachan (1993) created the *Basic Spelling Vocabulary List*, composed of 850 words categorized by grade level. These words make up 80 percent of words first through fifth graders use in their written expression. This spelling list is available for free on the Reading Rockets Web site at the following link: http://www .readingrockets.org/article/22366.

SPELLING INSTRUCTION: TIERS 2 AND 3

Errors in spelling tend to have regular patterns that can be related to difficulties with auditory discrimination or visual memory. Students with auditory discrimination problems may use incorrect consonant substitutions and confuse vowels because they cannot distinguish subtle differences between sounds. Possible indicators of visual memory problems may include reversing letters in words (the-hte), reversing entire words (man-nam), and spelling nonphonetic words phonetically (was-wuz). Students may also have difficulty remembering spelling patterns and applying spelling rules.

Students with auditory discrimination problems can benefit from additional phonemic awareness instruction (see Chapter 3). For example, they can practice segmenting words into sounds, and forming words by adding, taking away, or substituting sounds ("This word is *wide*, what's the word if we replaced the /w/ sound with /s/?"). Students receiving instruction in Tiers 2 and 3 will benefit from a personalized word list and self-selected goals for the number of words learned per week. When providing individualized instruction, use multisensory techniques (such as saying each letter, tracing each letter, manipulating letter tiles), emphasize spelling patterns (generating and sorting words by pattern), and limit the number of words taught each week. The following are recommended methods for students with spelling difficulties: Copy-Cover-Compare, Phonovisual Method, Simultaneous Oral Spelling Method, and the Horn Method.

Copy-cover-compare (Graham & Miller, 1979). This procedure requires students to examine a word as the teacher reads it, copy the word twice while looking at it, cover the word and write it from memory, check the spelling by comparing it to the model, and make corrections if necessary.

Phonovisual Method (Schoolfield & Timberlake, 1960). This is a phonetically-based approach emphasizing an association between a familiar visual image and the auditory letter sound (a picture of a dog presented when introducing the letter *d*). Consonants and vowels are introduced in this spelling method by association with word pictures that cue the visual image of the letter sound.

Simultaneous Oral Spelling Method (Gillingham & Stillman, 1970). This method uses a multisensory approach to teach correspondence between letters and sounds. The teacher systematically makes selections based on words the student has mastered and words the student needs to learn. The simultaneous oral spelling method emphasizes sound blending, repetition, and drill. The teacher says a word and the student repeats the word. Then the student says the sounds in the word and names the letters that represent each sound. Finally, the student writes the word while naming each letter.

Horn Method (Horn, 1954). This method requires the student to proceed through a sequence of steps: pronounce the word, look at each part of the word and repeat the pronunciation, spell the word orally, visualize the word and respell it orally, write the word, and check the word for accuracy. If there are any errors made during any part of the sequence, the entire process is repeated. This method relies on visual memorization and recall.

WRITING PROCESS INSTRUCTION: TIER 1

As students work on increasing their handwriting, keyboarding, and spelling proficiency, they should be provided with opportunities to apply those essential skills to authentic writing tasks, beginning with writing words, then sentences, then paragraphs. As students get older, they will benefit most from instruction that allows them to produce varied and extended writing pieces. Producing longer writing pieces, such as narrative stories or informative essays, requires students to learn the writing process. The writing process consists of the following stages: planning, drafting, revising, editing, and publishing (Graves, 1994). In the planning stage students generate and organize their ideas. They translate their planning notes into sentences and paragraphs in the drafting stage. When revising, students make improvements to the content and flow of the writing piece not yet focusing on mechanical errors. During the editing stage, students identify and correct mechanical errors (spelling, punctuation). In the publishing stage, students focus on producing a final polished product and seeing its effects on real audiences (Alber-Morgan, Hessler, & Konrad, 2007).

Writer's workshop (Atwell, 1987). A popular Tier 1 approach for teaching the writing process, writer's workshop is ideal for inclusive classrooms because it encourages independence and critical thinking while providing a positive and supportive environment for developing writers of all ability levels. Common features of *writer's workshop* include mini-lessons (brief, explicit instruction of specific writing elements), sustained time to work on various writing tasks that are personally meaningful, frequent opportunities for collaborating and sharing with peers, and individual conferencing for guidance, performance feedback, and goal setting (Troia, Lin, Monroe,

& Cohen, 2009). During daily blocks of time devoted to writing, teachers can provide direct instruction of mechanical elements, text structures, and writing strategies to the whole class. Then students can immediately apply those skills to their own written expression. Each student should have a folder with a collection of "in progress" writing pieces at various stages of completion. After teacher-led instruction, students can work independently, with a peer, in a collaborative group, or with an adult on writing pieces of their own choosing. The following are activities for teaching the writing process and building writing skills.

Planning and Organization

During this stage, students identify topics of personal interest, generate and organize their ideas about the topic, and identify their audience and purpose. Teachers can use thought-provoking pictures, videos, literature, and discussion to help students make connections to their own background knowledge and generate writing ideas. The following activities can stimulate interest and motivate students to produce personally meaningful writing.

Pictures. Show students an interesting picture (photograph, painting, video) and lead a discussion about how the picture makes the students feel. Ask students to think and talk about how the picture reminds them of a personal experience. Have students participate in generating a list of vocabulary words related to the picture that they can use in their stories. Prompt students to make up sentences about the picture, encouraging vivid descriptions based on what they see. The sentences can be used to write a class story. After this exercise, students can come up with their own stories about the picture or select a different picture for their writing piece.

Story starters. Story starters are phrases or sentences intended to stimulate written expression. Story starters likely to produce more written expression are those that relate to the students' background knowledge and interests. For example, many students who live in coastal South Carolina probably have been to the beach, so the story starter, "One day at the beach..." is probably appropriate. If your students have never been to the beach, it will be difficult for them to write about it. If students are uninterested in the story starter, they should be provided with additional choices. Teachers can help students link their background knowledge to the story starter by engaging them in a discussion of their experiences related to the topic.

Visual imagery. Guiding students to think about descriptive details can be accomplished by using visual imagery. Have students close their eyes and imagine a situation they have likely encountered (such as waiting at the bus stop on a snowy day, flying a kite on a windy day, walking in the woods in autumn, going to the fair on a sweltering August day). Guide students to think about what they see, hear, smell, feel, and taste. When they open their eyes, guide them in generating descriptive sentences about their visual imagery. "The First House Memory" (Marchisan & Alber, 2001) is an example of an exercise designed to stimulate background knowledge. The teacher asks the students to close their eyes and think of a room in a house where something memorable happened. While the students' eyes are closed, the teacher verbally guides the students to think about what the room looks like, the sounds and smells in the room, and the people in the room (what they're saying, wearing, doing). After the students open their eyes, they can discuss their memories of the event, make up sentences, draw a picture of the memorable event, write planning notes, and write a story.

Literature. Literature can stimulate writing ideas and provide students with good models for various writing types, styles, and purposes (Mason & Graham, 2008). When introducing students to a different writing genre, teachers should point out the critical elements, provide guided practice for identifying those elements in other writing pieces, and have students apply those elements to their own work. For example, teachers can provide examples of how expository writing pieces are structured. The first paragraph contains an attention grabber, a rationale for the importance of the topic, and the main ideas of the essay. Each subsequent paragraph contains a main idea and supporting details that relate back to the theme of the paper. The concluding paragraph summarizes the main ideas. After having students read and/or listen to each of several expository writing pieces, teachers can explicitly point out the common structure of each piece and prompt students to imitate that structure in their own writing.

For narrative fiction, teachers can read various stories and have students identify the following critical elements: characters, setting, problem, actions, emotions, climax, and resolution. When students plan their own stories, they can be guided to think about and include each story element. Literature can also be used to inspire writing ideas. For example, after reading portions of *Tales of a Fourth Grade Nothing* (Blume, 1972), lead students to think about how their experiences with their siblings are similar to the children in the book. Students can also engage in the following writing activities in response to literature:

- Write an alternate ending to a narrative fiction story.
- Write a character analysis of the character you like or dislike the most.
- Write about a personal experience similar to that of the main character.
- Write about how two fiction stories are similar and different.
- Write an opinion piece about the meaning or message of a story.
- Write a different story using the same characters.
- Introduce students to reading passages that evoke different emotions, discuss how the authors used words to convey certain feelings, and have students practice writing paragraphs using similar techniques.

Brainstorming. After students have decided on a personally meaningful topic, the next step is to brainstorm their ideas. Explain to students that brainstorming is writing down as many things as you can about a topic, without judgment, to generate good ideas. Teachers can model brainstorming by selecting a topic (such as "Why dogs are good pets") and having students generate a list of ideas about the topic (always happy to see you, loyal, good companion, can do tricks, makes me laugh, fun to play Frisbee with, brings in the newspaper, protects the house, and so on). After the teacher and students generate a list, the teacher models and guides students in selecting the most important items, crossing out the items that do not belong, and organizing the sequence of how the information will be presented from most important to least important. After the teacher models brainstorming and organization, students can work in pairs or in small groups to practice brainstorming and organizing self-selected topics.

Graphic organizers. Students can use graphic organizers to structure their brainstorming ideas into specific categories and sequences. These tools provide a visual representation of how concepts relate to each other and are a guide for drafting the writing piece. Students can use the same graphic organizers illustrated in Chapter 3 as planning guides for their own narrative (Figure 3.4) or expository (Figure 3.5) writing pieces. The following are examples of other graphic organizers that can be used to plan and organize different kinds of writing: Figure 5.1 (compare/contrast), Figure 5.2 (opinion piece), and Figure 5.3 (descriptive writing).

Figure 5.1 Example of Compare/Contrast Graphic Organizer (Venn diagram)

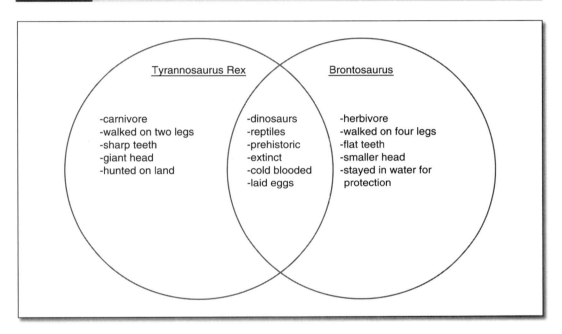

Figure 5.2 Example of Graphic Organizer for an Opinion Paper

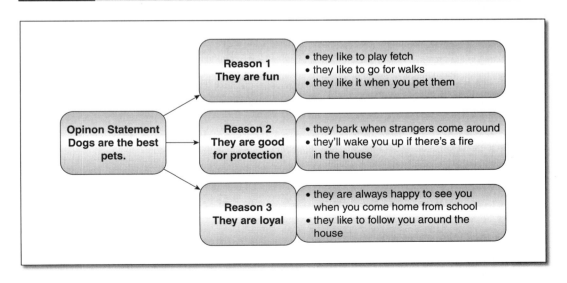

Figure 5.3   Graphic Organizer for Descriptive Writing

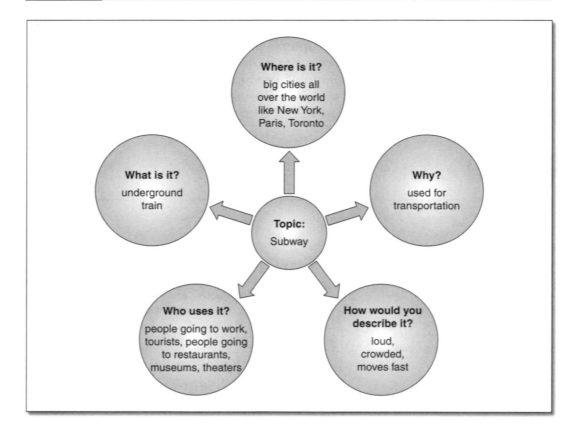

Collaborative planning. Students can work together in pairs or in small groups to select meaningful topics, brainstorm ideas, complete graphic organizers, and coauthor writing pieces. The following are two examples of how students can participate in collaborative planning for different kinds of writing. For opinion papers, Wong, Butler, Ficzere, and Kuperis (1996) had students work in pairs, each student taking a different side of an issue (for example, dress codes). Students wrote down their supporting arguments on planning sheets and discussed their arguments with their partners. During the discussion, the students asked for further explanation, clarification, and elaboration of their viewpoints. Wong, Butler, Ficzere, and Kuperis (1997) used a similar procedure to guide students in writing compare-contrast essays. Students worked in pairs to select a topic (such as concerts) and two categories of the topic to compare and contrast (like rock concerts versus school concerts). Students then brainstormed features of the topic they would discuss (goal, content, dress, demeanor). For each feature selected, the students listed details and indicated whether each detail was a similarity or difference.

Drafting

During the drafting stage of the writing process, students translate their planning notes into sequential sentences and paragraphs. Students should not worry about mechanical errors on early drafts because that may interfere with flow of ideas and writing production. Be clear that the content is the most important part of the writing piece, and that students will go back and fix all of the mistakes later. In order to teach students drafting skills, teachers should model and provide guided practice before having students work independently.

Teachers should use chart paper or an overhead projector to model translating planning notes into text. Figure 5.1 shows an example of a completed graphic organizer for a compare-contrast piece about two different dinosaurs. The teacher can use a graphic organizer like this and guide students through forming sentences. For example, "Look at the Venn diagram we made showing how the T-Rex and the Brontosaurus are alike and how they are different. Let's think of a first sentence that introduces the reader to what you are going to talk about." The teacher calls on a student who says, "The Tyrannosaurus Rex and Brontosaurus were dinosaurs that had many similarities and differences." The teacher provides feedback, writes the sentence on the chart paper, and continues guiding the students to generate additional sentences by referring to the graphic organizer ("T-Rex and Brontosaurus were both big, hungry reptiles, but T-Rex was a carnivore and Brontosaurus was an herbivore."). After this exercise, students can practice drafting sentences using their own graphic organizers. They can work individually, with a peer, or in a cooperative learning group. Just as students can engage in collaborative planning and organization, they can also participate in collaborative drafting. Pairs of students can sit together at a computer and take turns creating sentences from their planning notes. Collaborative writing has been demonstrated to improve the quality and production of written expression, especially for low-achieving students (MacArthur, 2009).

An important concern during the drafting stage is writing fluency. If students are fluent writers, they will have an easier time drafting their writing pieces. In order to increase fluency in general, students should be engaged in frequent writing activities throughout the day and across the curriculum. For example, students can write brief reactions to reading passages, summaries for different content-area reading passages, story problems for math, critiques of stories or movies, test questions for science and social studies units, directions for solving a problem or playing a game, captions for pictures, or a dialogue between two historical figures. Additionally, students can write brief daily journal entries on self-selected or teacher-selected topics. Another way to increase writing fluency is having students participate in repeated writings. This is similar to repeated readings. Students rewrite the same passage two or three times during one- to three-minute timed trials. With each successive timed trial, students attempt to increase the number of words written per minute.

A useful tool for increasing fluency during the drafting stage is the use of word banks. Teachers and students can develop various word banks to support drafting. Word banks can be individualized lists based on students' writing needs and attached to individual writing folders. Teachers can also have the whole class generate word banks on the board for specific writing activities ("Before you write your Halloween stories, let's write some Halloween words on the board.") The following are examples of word lists that may be helpful to students during drafting: adjectives and adverbs, action verbs, transition words and phrases, frequently misspelled words, and self-selected words.

Revising/Editing

During the revising stage, students critically examine their writing for clarity, completeness, and sequential flow. After the revising stage, students begin the editing stage, in which they focus on correcting mechanical errors (such as spelling or punctuation). Students need to understand that revising and editing are an integral part of the writing process and necessary for producing high-quality work. Error-monitoring checklists, peer editing, and mini-lessons are Tier 1 approaches to teaching revising and editing.

Error-monitoring checklists. Because revising and editing can be overwhelming for students, they should only focus on a few skills at a time. Students can keep individualized editing and revising checklists in their folders and use them as a guide to correct their errors. For example, a lower-performing student may have the following items on his or her checklist: (a) I wrote my name on my paper, (b) I indented the first sentence, and (c) I started each sentence with a capital letter. Additional items can be gradually added to individualized checklists as the student attains mastery of easier editing skills. For example, (a) I capitalized proper nouns, (b) I put the correct punctuation at the end of each sentence, (c) I used correct subject/verb agreement, and (d) I used correct spelling.

Peer editing. Peer editing is a particularly effective strategy for improving writing proficiency as well as motivation. Students can work together in pairs to read or listen to each other's stories, say what they liked about the writing piece, ask questions for clarification, provide suggestions, and edit for mechanical errors. Figure 5.4 shows an example of a peer revising form. Students can respond to the prompts on the form in order to provide each other with feedback. Prior to implementing a peer-editing arrangement, teachers should model, role-play, and provide practice of rules for giving and receiving feedback. For example, students should practice listening carefully, communicating in a positive way, and accepting feedback politely.

Mini-lessons. A key component of writer's workshop is using mini-lessons to teach editing skills. During mini-lessons, teachers provide direct instruction of writing elements based on an analysis of student writing errors. For example, after examining writing samples, the teacher realizes that most of the students need to learn how to punctuate direct quotes. She uses sentences from student work samples, writes them on the board, then models and demonstrates how to correct them. Students can practice several examples of the skill by writing on their response boards. Mini-lessons can be used to teach students a range of editing and revising skills. Teachers can also provide students with additional daily opportunities to practice editing and revising by writing a different sentence on the board with multiple mechanical errors. Have the students rewrite the sentence with the errors corrected, and then go over each correction. As students become more proficient with editing, more challenging errors can be gradually added to the daily sentence.

Sentence revision. Teachers can use the following practice activities to help students with sentence revision. Read several examples of interesting sentences from children's literature to the students. For example,

| Figure 5.4 | Example of Peer-Revising Form |

Author Directions	**Peer Editor Directions**
Title _____	Title _____
Author _____	Author _____
Peer Editor _____	Peer Editor _____
Directions to Author:	Directions to Peer Editor:
1. Read your story aloud to your peer while he or she follows along.	1. Listen carefully and follow along while the author reads.
2. Listen attentively to your peer's feedback.	2. Think about what you like about the story and what might improve the story.
3. Politely accept feedback and ask questions to make sure you understand.	3. Tell your peer at least two things you liked about the story.
4. Write down the suggestions you might want to use on your revision.	4. Tell your peer one thing that might improve the story.
5. Say thank you.	5. Say thank you.
Author's notes:	Editor's Notes:
Possible revisions to make:	What I liked:
_____	_____
_____	_____
_____	_____
_____	_____
_____	One suggestion:
_____	_____
_____	_____
_____	_____

"Mr. Seahorse drifted gently through the sea, he passed right by a group of trumpet fish hidden in a patch of reeds" (Carle, 2004, pp. 4–5). Then guide the students to identify what makes each sentence interesting (vivid description, action verbs, rhythm, or sentence structure). Next, present a brief and uninteresting sentence ("The girl left the park."). Discuss with students that the sentence is boring because there is not enough description, then model ways to make the sentence more interesting by using adjectives, action verbs, and elaborating on details ("The nervous girl hurried away from the desolate and smelly park downtown."). Students can practice elaborating on sentences by writing on their response cards and sharing their revised sentences with the class.

Students can also practice elaborating sentences in the context of a story. Take a series of sequential uninteresting story sentences (for example: 1. I have a dog; 2. He has fleas; 3. My brother gave the dog a bath; 4. The dog tried to get away, and so on.), and read them to the class. Lead a discussion about how the story could be much more interesting. Then provide each student or pair of students with a different sentence to revise. When the students are finished, prompt them to read their sentences when you say their numbers (*Number 1:* "I have a big friendly dog who likes to roll in the mud." *Number 2:* "His itchy flea bites made him so miserable."). Discuss how the new revised story is different from the first story.

Publishing

The culminating product of the writing process is publication—sharing the writing piece with others. During this stage, students focus on polishing their work and taking pride in being an author. Publishing is an effective and motivating way to give writing an authentic purpose, and results in improvement in the quality of narrative and informative writing (MacArthur, Graham, Schwartz, & Schafer, 1995). Posting stories on bulletin boards is one popular and simple way to publish student work. Teachers can also publish student writing in classroom newspapers, newsletters, or Web sites. "Author's chair" is another form of publication in which students read their stories aloud to the class. Students can also create their own books—hard copy or electronic.

WRITING PROCESS INSTRUCTION: TIERS 2 AND 3

Many of the writing activities mentioned before can also be used for more intensive supplemental instruction with small groups or individuals needing extra support with planning, drafting, revising, and editing. For example, after the teacher delivers a whole-class mini-lesson of a specific skill (like using commas), she can provide additional instruction and guided practice to a small group of students who need extra help. The teacher can also provide individual assistance by conferencing and cowriting with students. During individual conferences, the teacher listens and offers support, encouragement, and constructive criticism. Conferencing should be used to foster development of ideas, planning, writing, revising, and editing (Mason & Graham, 2008). Through questioning, teachers can help students gain more insight into using the writing process to accomplish specific goals.

Cowriting can be used to support initial writing attempts and ongoing writing development. Assistance is gradually faded as the student becomes more independent, and this is called scaffolding. With cowriting, the teacher and student sit side by side at the computer. The teacher may start by typing sentences the student says, then having the student type some sentences when he or she is ready. The teacher and student can collaborate on the story, with the teacher typing the beginning and middle parts and the student typing the ending. Gradually, the student takes over writing whole stories, with reduced dependence on the teacher for support and guidance. The cowriting strategy can also be used to help students revise and edit their work. The teacher can provide guidance for determining if sentences make sense, elaborating on important details, and monitoring for mechanical errors.

For students struggling with written expression, commercial direct instruction (DI) writing programs are available (such as *Expressive Writing, Language for Learning*). DI writing programs use the same model, lead, and test sequence used in DI reading programs. For example, *Expressive Writing* (Engelmann & Silbert, 1983) provides sequenced instruction with frequent practice and review in sentence writing, paragraph writing, revising, and editing. Students build prerequisite writing skills before applying them to new tasks. Critical features of the program are systematic presentation, frequent practice, and frequent review of grammar, usage, and punctuation.

Summarizing strategy. Practice with summary writing is an evidence-based practice for increasing both reading comprehension and writing skills (Graham & Perin, 2007). The *GIST strategy* (Rhoder, 2002) is a good activity for teaching students to summarize. Students read an article and answer *who, what, when, where, why* and *how* questions. Students then compact the information down to 20 words. Teachers should encourage students to make several revisions and carefully select the most accurate 20 words for the 20-word summary.

Another activity for helping students summarize is having them create a story board (DiSpirt, 2008). Have students fold a piece of paper in half the long way and then into thirds so there are six squares. Each square represents part of a reading passage. Have students number each square from one to six. After reading a passage, have the students write a sentence in the first square that tells the beginning. Then fill in the last square to tell the ending. Students can work together or independently to figure out what goes in the squares in between. After the graphic organizer is complete, students can use it to write their summaries, and then share their summaries with small or large groups.

Writing Strategies

Explicit instruction of writing strategies enables students to self-regulate their writing to accomplish specific goals (Baker, Gersten, & Graham, 2003). Strategy instruction is comprised of implementing self-regulating procedures required to independently complete a task. A mnemonic device is usually used to prompt the student through each step of the writing task. For example, DEFENDS (Ellis & Friend, 1991) is a mnemonic strategy for writing an opinion paper. The steps are as follows: **D**ecide on your exact position, **E**xamine the reasons for your position, **F**orm a list of points that explain each reason, **E**xpose your position in the first sentence, **N**ote each reason for supporting points, **D**rive home the position in the last sentence, **S**earch for errors and correct.

Teachers can use Self-Regulated Strategy Development (SRSD; Graham & Harris, 2005) to teach students to use specific writing strategies (like DEFENDS). Decades of research on SRSD has demonstrated substantial gains for struggling writers in both elementary and secondary classrooms, including students with learning disabilities, students with intellectual disabilities, and English language learners (Graves & Rueda, 2009). Graham and Harris (2005) describe the following steps for implementing SRSD:

1. *Develop and activate background knowledge.* Students read examples of the genre they will be writing and teachers make sure students have the prerequisite skills to learn the strategy (such as knowledge of specific story elements).

2. *Discuss the strategy.* The teacher describes the strategy and its benefits, discusses how and when it should be used, and obtains the student's commitment to learn the strategy.

3. *Model the strategy.* The teacher models and describes each step of the strategy by using a "think aloud" procedure.

4. *Memorize the strategy.* The student memorizes the strategy steps and self-instructions using a cue card as an aid.

5. *Support the strategy.* The teacher and student collaboratively use the strategy to produce or edit a composition. Initially, the teacher provides more support, prompts, and guidance. As the student becomes more proficient with using the strategy, the teacher gradually withdraws support until the student can use the strategy independently.

6. *Independent performance.* The student performs the strategy independently with teacher support as needed. Programming for maintenance and generalization also occurs during this step.

There are many self-regulation strategies that can help students produce writing for different purposes. Selection of a learning strategy should be based on the needs of individual learners and the usefulness of the strategy across situations. When modeling the strategy and guiding practice, teachers should keep the wording clear and simple, adapt the strategy for individual differences, and apply the strategy to personally meaningful writing topics. Additionally, students will need frequent guided and independent practice using the strategy. Table 5.1 shows examples of writing strategies for different purposes.

Table 5.1   Writing Strategies

Strategy	Mnemonic Steps
PLEASE (Welch, 1992) *Paragraph Writing*	**P**ick the topic, audience, and paragraph type (such as compare/contrast). **L**ist information about the topic. **E**valuate whether the list is complete and determine order. **A**ctivate your writing by starting with a topic sentence. **S**upply supporting or detail sentences, using items from the list. **E**nd with a strong concluding sentence.
WWW,What-2, How-2 (Graham & Harris, 1992) *Narrative Writing*	WWW: Who? (is the main character), When? (does it take place), Where? (does it take place) What-2: What? (does the main character want to do); What? (happens when she does it) How-2: How? (does it end), How? (does the character feel?)

Strategy	Mnemonic Steps
C-SPACE (Graham & Harris, 1992) *Narrative*	**C**haracter, **S**etting, **P**roblem, **A**ctions, **C**onclusion, **E**motion
TREE (Graham & Harris, 1989) *Opinion Writing*	**T**opic sentence **R**easons to support premise **E**xamine soundness of each reason **E**nding
STOP-DARE (De La Paz & Graham, 1997) *Opinion Writing*	**S**uspend judgment **D**evelop a topic sentence **T**ake a side **A**dd supporting ideas **O**rganize ideas **R**eject possible arguments for the other side **P**lan more as you write **E**nd with a conclusion
TOWER (Schumaker, 2003) *Expository Writing*	**T**hink about the content **O**rder topics and details **W**rite the rough draft, look for **E**rrors **R**evise and **R**ewrite
SCORE A (Korinek & Bulls, 1996) *Expository Writing*	**S**elect a topic **C**reate categories **O**btain reference tools **R**ead and take notes **E**venly organize information using note cards **A**pply writing process
COPS (Schumaker et al., 1985) *Editing*	**C**apitalization **O**verall appearance **P**unctuation **S**pelling
CDO (Graham, 1997) *Revising*	**C**ompare—Does my sentence match what I really wanted to say? **D**iagnose—Select problem from a diagnostic card (such as lacks detail) **O**perate—After rewriting the sentence, was the change effective? Process is repeated at paragraph level
SEARCH (Ellis & Friend, 1991) *Revising and Editing*	**S**et goals **E**xamine paper to see if it makes sense **A**sk if you said what you meant **R**eveal picky errors **C**opy over neatly **H**ave a last look for errors

COMPUTER TECHNOLOGY FOR WRITING: TIER 1

Research demonstrates that students produce longer and higher-quality compositions when they use computer technology for writing (Goldberg, Russell, & Cook, 2003; Graham & Perin, 2007). Additionally, using word-processing programs has resulted in increased revisions, reduced errors, and better attitudes toward writing (Sturm, Rankin, Beukelman, & Schultz-Muehling, 1997). Word-processing programs allow students to make frequent revisions without tiresome recopying, correct errors without messy erasing, and produce neatly printed work (MacArthur, 1996). The visibility of the text on the screen can be useful for facilitating collaborative writing between peers. Another benefit of visibility is that teacher can easily observe student writing processes and provide instructional feedback (MacArthur).

An excellent tool for whole-class writing instruction is an interactive whiteboard. This is a large dry-erase board on which a projector displays a computer's desktop. The whiteboard functions as a large touch screen. Text and illustrations can be manipulated on the screen using electronic pens or fingers. Any work completed on the whiteboard can be captured and modified electronically. An interactive whiteboard can be used to demonstrate how to use the computer to produce and edit written expression (keyboarding, formatting, copying, pasting, using spell check, saving text, using the thesaurus and dictionary). It can also be used to model and guide students through the writing process. For example, during planning, teachers can use the whiteboard to create brainstorming lists and complete graphic organizers. Teachers can also demonstrate how to create sentences from planning notes, revise for content, and edit for mechanical errors. The whiteboard can be used to teach students how to do an Internet search and demonstrate how to use software. For example, *REfworks* (ProQuest) and *EndNote* (Thompson ResearchSoft, 2008) are software programs that provide students with assistance with collecting and formatting references and creating bibliographies.

Whiteboards can also be used to demonstrate how to use multimedia programs that integrate drawing tools, video, and sound. These kinds of programs can be motivating for all developing writers. They can be especially useful for culturally and linguistically diverse students who may have limited background knowledge. Additionally, multimedia programs may enable culturally diverse students to select visuals and sounds that have personal significance for them.

The *Amazing Writing Machine* (Riverdeep Inc.) is an example of multimedia program that guides students through the writing process. Students begin with the "Project Picker," in which they select from five projects (essay, letter, story, poem, or journal). They can then decide to write from scratch or work on editing and customizing a prewritten outline. Other features include "Bright Ideas" (guides students in brainstorming and generating ideas), "Infosaurus" (finds words), "Reader Robot" (reads the story back to the student in one of eight voices), "Illustrating" (provides drawing, painting, rubber stamps, and clip art), and "Publishing" (prints story in various formats including fold-up books). Other examples of similar multimedia writing programs include *Kids Media Magic* and *Storybook Weaver.*

COMPUTER TECHNOLOGY FOR WRITING: TIERS 2 AND 3

Computer technology offers many levels of support for students needing more intensive instruction. Word prediction software, text-to-speech, and speech-to-text features are available in many programs to help students with planning, organization, and revising as they move through the writing process.

Planning and organization software can assist students by prompting them for specific information or presenting a series of response prompts for composing stories. *Inspiration* (for Grades 6–12) and *Kidspiration* (for Grades K–5) are examples of programs that can help students plan their compositions by helping them create semantic maps that can automatically be turned into an outline. Other examples of programs useful for planning and organization include *Kid Pix* (Riverdeep Inc.), *Storybook Weaver* (Riverdeep Inc.), and *Draft: Builder* (Don Johnston Inc.).

Programs that contain word prediction and word banks can be very helpful for struggling writers. For example, with *Co:Writer 4000* (Don Johnston Inc.), as each letter is typed, a series of words with the same beginning letters appear on the screen. The student clicks on the intended word when it appears. This program also includes speech synthesis so the student can hear whether or not he selected the intended word. Other examples of word prediction software with speech synthesis include *Word Q Writing Aid Software* (Quillsoft) and *Kid Works 2* (Riverdeep Inc.).

Text-to-speech technology allows students to hear what they have written so they can more easily evaluate the correctness of their writing (MacArthur, 1996). Discrepancies between what students have written and what they intended to express are more easily detected. Examples of text-to-speech writing programs include *Write Outloud* (Riverdeep Inc.) and *Read and Write Gold* (Brighteye Technology). Both of these programs include text-to-speech, speech-to-text, and word prediction.

Voice-recognition programs allow students to produce written expression by speaking into a microphone while the computer types what is said. These speech-to-text programs help students who have severe motor or writing production problems. Although each program must be calibrated to a specific voice, once calibrated, the software is quite reliable in recording the correct words. Examples of speech-to-text software include *Dragon NaturallySpeaking* (Nuance), *Windows Vista Speech Recognition*, *IBM ViaVoice 10 Standard*, and *MacSpeech Dictate*. Computer technology can provide many levels of support in inclusive classrooms.

SUMMARY

The ability to produce quality writing opens doors to many opportunities for enriching experiences. In addition to being a very important tool for learning and communicating, writing is also a highly regarded outlet for creativity. Far too many students lack motivation to write because it can be such a struggle. However, when teachers plan multitiered instruction using evidence-based practices, students with a history of failure can become successful and inspired. Authentic and personally meaningful writing tasks are more likely to motivate effortful writing. In order to focus clearly on their flow of ideas, students will need to have adequate transcription skills such as handwriting, keyboarding, and spelling. Tier 1 approaches for transcription skills include direct instruction and frequent opportunities for active responding and specific feedback. Students needing more intensive instruction can benefit from various forms of multisensory instruction, self-correction, and additional practice.

In addition to transcription skills, students also need to be able to plan, organize, and write different kinds of compositions. Teaching the writing process is an evidence-based practice for increasing writing quality and proficiency. Writer's workshop provides flexible and differentiated Tier 1 instruction for teaching the writing process. In writer's workshop, students can work independently or with peers on a variety of writing pieces. Writer's workshop encourages students to make choices, engage in personally meaningful writing, and set their own goals. Supplemental writing process instruction at Tiers 2 and 3 should include direct instruction of writing strategies because of their effectiveness for struggling writers. With strategy instruction, students memorize a mnemonic for producing a specific type of writing (such as DEFENDS for persuasive papers). Each letter in the mnemonic represents each sequential step for the writing piece. Teachers can use Self-Regulated Strategy Development (SRSD; Graham & Harris, 2005) to teach students different writing strategies. When teaching the writing process, students at all instructional tiers will benefit from the flexibility and support of computer technology. For example, teachers can use interactive white boards to provide Tier 1 instruction. Additionally, computer technology offers a wide range of support for students with physical, intellectual, or learning disabilities (voice recognition, word prediction) as well as for typically developing and gifted students (multimedia writing programs).

CARMEN

Carmen looked through her writing folder to decide which story she wanted to work on. She shuffled through the different planning notes and drafts until she found the story she started called "Honey Island Swamp." She was excited about working on this story today because her teacher was going to help her get started on the revisions.

"Did you decide which story you wanted to work on?" asked Mr. Blake.

"Yes. It's called "Honey Island Swamp.""

"Oh, I think that will be a good one to work on. Read to me what you have so far."

Carmen began reading, "Last summer I went to visit my cousin in Louisiana and we took a boat-ride tour through the swamp. We saw a lot of cool plants and animals, but this was the coolest thing that happened. The man who was driving the boat made a sound to call the alligators. Then five baby alligators came to the boat and ate marshmallows. My cousin told me that some people think Big Foot lives in Honey Island Swamp but Big Foot isn't real."

"That's a good start," said Mr. Blake, "One thing you want to do is give the reader a clear picture of what you experienced. How can you do that?"

"Describe more of what I saw and heard?" Carmen asked.

"Good, tell me what you can add to your story."

"Like, there were trees in the water that were really fat on the bottom part of the trunk and we could hear all different kinds of birds and bugs singing and chirping and," Carmen remembered something important, "it was really . . . really . . . really . . . hot!"

"Those are really important details to add, very good." Mr. Blake prompted Carmen to jot those notes down so she would remember to add those details to the story later. To provide a model, he also helped Carmen work through revising one of the sentences.

"Carmen," said Mr. Blake, "let's look at the sentence, 'Then five baby alligators came to the boat and ate marshmallows.' How did the baby alligators come to the boat?"

"They didn't splash, they just moved in a smooth way, they didn't flap their legs, they just kept them straight."

"Good, now how did they eat the marshmallows?"

By asking Carmen questions that helped her elaborate on the details, Carmen understood what she needed to do to make this story better. She proudly read the revised sentence about the alligators to Mr. Blake.

"Five baby alligators glided toward the boat with just their heads out of the water and their jaws open. When the tour guide threw marshmallows in the water, the alligators let the marshmallows float into their mouths and gently closed their jaws." After receiving positive feedback and encouragement from Mr. Blake, Carmen continued working on her revisions until the recess bell rang.

6

Integrating Language Arts Across the Curriculum With Thematic Units

Considering the logical connections between reading and writing, it makes sense to teach them together in a unified context rather than teaching skills in isolation of one another. Combining reading and writing instruction has resulted in positive outcomes for diverse learners acquiring and maintaining a variety of literacy skills (Foorman et al., 2006; Shanahan, 2009; Thames et al., 2008). For example, Thames and colleagues (2008) examined the effects of individualized integrated language arts instruction on the reading performance of fourth through eighth graders. Integrated language arts instruction, which consisted of listening, speaking, reading, and writing, resulted in significant increases in reading comprehension for struggling readers. Similarly, Stevens (2006) found that integrating reading and writing instruction for middle school students improved their reading comprehension as well as their vocabulary proficiency and written expression.

Teachers can use the obvious connections between reading and writing to increase instructional efficiency, generalization, and student learning (Shanahan, 2009). For example, teaching spelling in connection with decoding is an efficient and effective way to improve basic reading and writing skills (Coker, 2006). Teachers can also link reading comprehension instruction with writing. Reading selections used for comprehension instruction can also be used as models for students producing written expression with the same text structure.

In addition to supporting connected reading and writing instruction, research also supports integrating reading and writing skills into content-area instruction (such as social studies, science). Integrating language arts instruction across the curriculum throughout the school day provides frequent practice with literacy skills and opportunities to program for and assess generalization. Additionally, students demonstrate improved achievement with both literacy skills and content-area knowledge (Hand, Hohenshell, & Prain, 2004; Morrow, Pressley, Smith, & Smith, 1997). For example, the research of Morrow and colleagues (1997) demonstrated that integrating literacy instruction with science content in diverse third grade classrooms resulted in significant increased proficiency with both literacy skills and science concepts.

A good way to combine language arts and content-area instruction in inclusive classrooms is planning and implementing thematic units. With thematic units, teachers design instruction across the curriculum around a central theme (like the rain forest). This approach allows students to practice literacy skills across connected contexts while building their background knowledge. This chapter provides teachers with guidelines and suggestions for planning relevant and effective thematic units that integrate language arts and content curriculum. In addition to incorporating much-needed frequent practice opportunities of literacy skills, these thematic units can be designed to support students' critical thinking, interactive learning, and creative expression while providing multitiered instruction for diverse learners.

CREATING THEMATIC UNITS FOR MULTITIERED INSTRUCTION

When general and special education teachers collaborate to plan thematic units for multitiered instruction, they can combine their unique skills and interests to create more vibrant instruction and varied learning opportunities. They can also model the collaboration skills that they will be expecting from their students. Several researchers and practitioners have recommended general procedures for developing thematic units (Barrentine, 1999; Ferguson, 2002). Most involve using some or all of the following planning steps in various sequences: selecting a theme, identifying goals, locating resources, planning learning activities, and determining assessments. Anderson and Anderson (2006) recommend identifying the final product of the thematic unit first (for instance, a presentation) and then planning instruction that enables students to produce that product. When teachers plan a thematic unit, they will probably find that the process is actually more recursive than sequential. That is, as teachers plan the unit, they may frequently return to previous steps in the planning process to revise resources, activities, or accommodations. The following section provides teachers with a general framework for creating thematic units. Figure 6.1 is an example of a planning sheet that teachers may use or adapt to help guide them through the process.

Figure 6.1   Thematic Unit Planning Sheet

Theme: Africa	
Reading Materials and Resources	

Literature Folktales	**Social Studies** Culture, History, Geography, Economy
Abiyoyo by Pete Seeger *How the Ostrich Got Its Long Neck; A Tale from the Akamba of Kenya* by Marcia Brown *Koi and the Kola Nuts: A Tale from Liberia* by Joe Cepeda *Oh, Kojo! How Could You!: An Ashanti Tale* by Marc Brown *Makwelane and the Crocodile* by Maria Hendricks *Mufaro's Beautiful Daughters* by John Steptoe	*Africa* by David Petersen *Africa Is Not a Country* by Margy Burns Knight & Mark Melnicove *Ashanti to Zulu: African Traditions* by Margaret Musgrove *Jambo Means Hello* by Muriel Feelings *Look What Came From Africa* by Miles Harvey *Master Weaver from Ghana* by Gilbert Ahiagble & Louise Meyer
Science Climate, Plants, and Animals	**Math** Concepts, Applications
Serengeti Journey: On Safari in Africa by Gare Thompson *Along the Luangwa: A Story of an African Floodplain* by Schuyler Bull *Calabash Cat and His Amazing Journey* by James Rumford *Owen & Mzee: The True Story of a Remarkable Friendship* by IsabellaHatkoff, Craig Hatkoff, & Paula Kahumu	*Africa Counts: Number and Pattern in African Cultures* by Claudia Zaslavsky *Moja Means One, Swahili Counting Book* by Muriel Feelings *Emeka's Gift: An African Counting Story* by Ifeoma Onyefulu
Art/Music Visual Arts	**Physical Education** Dance
Hands-On Africa: Art Activities for All Ages by Yvonne Y. Merrill & Mary Simpson *The Tribal Arts of Africa* by Jean-Baptiste Bacquart *African Masks* by Iris Hahner, Maria Kecskesi, & Lazlo Vajda *The Rough Guide to African Music for Children CD* by Children for Children	*West African Drum & Dance* by Kalani & Ryan M. Camara *Drumbeat in Our Feet* by Patricia A. Keeler & Julio Leitao *Joneeba! The African Dance Workout* by A. Djoniba Mouflet, Mali M. Fleming, Lara Anasaze MS, & Misani

Language Arts Skills	
Listening: • listening to word pronunciations and decoding rules • listening to new vocabulary, definitions, examples • listening to peers read to provide error correction during peer tutoring • listening to teacher read the story, listen to comprehension questions, listen to peers' ideas in cooperative learning groups • listening to directions for how to plan and draft writing pieces, listen to peer feedback during peer editing groups	Speaking • pronouncing words, state decoding rules • stating vocabulary definitions, say words in context, make up sentences • providing verbal feedback, praise, and error correction during paired reading • asking and answering questions, retelling, summarizing • providing peer feedback during peer editing, discussing writing ideas and goals • acting out skits

(Continued)

Figure 6.1 (Continued)

Reading	Writing
• reading vocabulary words in isolation and in context • paired reading, repeated reading, choral reading • reading directions, and comprehension questions • reading a range of texts (narrative, informative, persuasive) from a range of sources (books, newspaper, Internet) • reading and self-regulating written expression • reading peers' written expression	• writing vocabulary words in sentences (e.g., on paper, on response cards) • writing semantic maps using vocabulary words • writing the answers to questions, summaries • writing test questions • writing planning notes, drafting, revising, editing • writing stories, opinion pieces, compare-contrast essays

Part 1	Part 2	Part 3	Part 4	Part 5
Geography, Demographics Climate: grasslands, jungle, desert, subarctic Folk tales by region Zimbabwe: *Mufaro's Beautiful Daughters* by John Steptoe	Early Civilization (pyramids, stone circles) Grassland carnivores and herbivores Folktale *Koi and the Kola Nuts: A Tale from Liberia* by Joe Cepeda	Pre-colonial Africa Jungle animals (primates, snakes, crocodiles) Folktale: *Makwelane and the Crocodile* by Maria Hendricks	Slave trade, Colonialism, Independence Desert animals (lizards, scorpions), Folktale: *Oh, Kojo! How Could You!: An Ashanti Tale* by Marc Brown	Current events Visual arts Music (influence on modern music), dance, sports (soccer, cricket) Folktale: *Abiyoyo* by Pete Seeger

Part 1: Multitiered Activities

Tier 1 Activities

Language Arts

Introduce new vocabulary from *Mufaro's Beautiful Daughters*

Read story aloud to students, have them "think-pair-share" to answer questions, make predictions, complete a story map, retell

Paired reading (provide choice of topic-related books at appropriate differentiated reading levels)

Writing: Compare/Contrast Essays, choice: compare and contrast the two sisters, compare and contrast this story to Cinderella, compare/contrast to a self-selected story

Enrichment: Opinion paper, What is beauty?

Content Areas

Introduce vocabulary and concepts for *Serengeti Journey: On Safari in Africa*, use a KWL chart to introduce book.

Have students read and practice summarizing main ideas, completing a main idea map, write test questions

Have students complete guided notes on introductory African geography and different climate regions, work in groups to begin researching a topic for oral presentations.

Writing: Find pictures on the Internet or in books and write descriptions of selected African animals.

Tiers 2 and 3 Activities

Language Arts

Supplemental decoding and vocabulary practice, Reading practice with rhyming books, *Bringing the Rain to Kapiti Plane* by Beatriz Vidal and *Off to the Sweet Shores of Africa and Other Talking Drum Rhymes*

Repeated readings with self-graphing

Co-writing with the teacher

Content Area

Additional practice with vocabulary, keyword method, semantic mapping

Study strategies, highlighting text, structured self-questioning, listening to tape-recorded text

Accommodations: modified guided notes, high interest-low vocabulary reading choices, tape-recorded reading passages, assistive technology, peer buddy, additional audio/visual materials, assistive technology with word processing (e.g., speech-to-text, text-to-speech, word prediction), supplement instruction with text in native language, picture-based software programs, self-monitoring tools, additional prompts, simplified directions, pencil grips, slant boards, reduce amount of reading, modify pace, minimize distractions, provide short breaks, oral responding for assessment, break large assignments down into manageable chunks

SELECTING A THEME

Teachers are more likely to design relevant and motivating thematic units when they consider the range of their students' unique backgrounds, abilities, and needs. Prior to planning the thematic unit, teachers can provide students with opportunities to describe their diverse backgrounds and express their interests either through writing (with surveys or open-ended questions) or through discussion (whole class, small group, and/or individual). Teachers can also obtain information about student backgrounds and interests by talking to parents or asking parents to complete a survey. The survey may contain questions such as: What does your child like to do during his or her free time? What is your child's favorite book? Who are your child's heroes? What activities does your child enjoy? Information derived from these kinds of questions will help teachers plan meaningful instruction and program for generalization.

The cultural diversity of the students in the inclusive classroom can be a source of relevant and content-rich themes. In addition to providing direction for topic selection, cultural diversity should also be considered when planning instructional delivery. For example, many culturally and linguistically diverse students attain better achievement when they participate in cooperative learning groups (Gersten et al., 2007). With this in mind, teachers can include several cooperative learning activities as integral parts of the thematic unit.

Another important consideration regarding student needs is the range of academic skill levels in the inclusive classroom. Some students will need more practice and small-group remediation with specific literacy skills, while more advanced students may need enrichment. Additionally, the students with disabilities will need the accommodations delineated in their IEPs. Organizing this information and having it available during planning will help guide teachers through the process of selecting appropriate materials and structuring appropriate learning activities.

Collaborative brainstorming is a good way to begin the process of identifying student needs and selecting a meaningful theme. Themes should be designed to integrate language arts skills with content, build upon previous learning, incorporate multicultural perspectives, and consider the interests of the local community (Barrentine, 1999). Most important, the theme should capture students' interest and increase their motivation to learn about the topic through verbal interaction, inquiry, problem solving, reading, and writing (Barrentine).

For the sake of efficiency with instructional time, teachers should attempt to link students' interests with state standards and benchmarks when selecting a theme (Bolak, Bialach, & Dunphy, 2005). For example, an Ohio third-grade social studies standard is "Citizenship Rights and Responsibilities," and a third-grade technology standard is "Technology and Society

Interaction," with a benchmark of "Define responsible citizenship relative to technology." Additionally, under the science and technology standard, one of the benchmarks is, "Describe ways that using technology can have helpful and/or harmful results and investigate ways that the results of technology may affect the individual, family and community" (Ohio Department of Education, 2009). In addition to covering state standards across at least three content areas, connecting citizenship rights to technology can provide a very interesting thematic unit that encourages opportunities for critical thinking while allowing students frequent practice of literacy skills. Meinbach, Fredericks, and Rothlein (2000) suggest the following possible theme categories: curricular topics (such as seasons, body systems), issues (rules, homework), problems (food shortage, ozone layer), special events (holidays, elections), and literary interests (poetry, science fiction).

After brainstorming a list of possible themes, teachers can examine their topics, eliminate the least feasible or relevant topics, identify the most interesting and useful topics, and sequence them according to preference. Conducting an Internet search of the top few themes may help teachers make their decision. This preliminary search may also lead to especially interesting books, materials, or ideas that can provide good directions for the theme.

Teachers can then begin organizing the unit by either creating a book web or a theme web (Meinbach et al., 2000). With book webbing, cross curricular instruction is designed around a piece of literature. For example, Figure 6.2

| Figure 6.2 | Book Web for Planning a Thematic Unit |

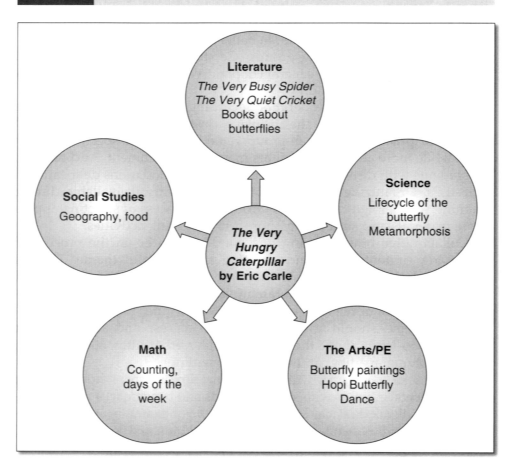

shows the connections of *The Very Hungry Caterpillar* by Eric Carle to science, social studies, math, other literature, and the arts. With theme webbing, cross-curricular instruction is designed around a topic or theme. Figure 6.3 shows an example of a theme web that identifies topics connected to Africa.

Figure 6.3 Example of a Theme Web for Planning a Thematic Unit

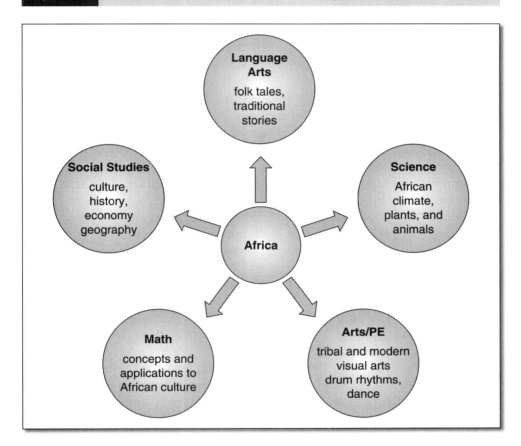

IDENTIFYING AND OBTAINING RESOURCES AND MATERIALS

Once general topics are identified, teachers will have better direction for obtaining resources. Several resources and materials may have already been identified during the initial search for theme ideas. When gathering instructional materials, teachers should consider student reading levels, cultural backgrounds, individual interests, age appropriateness, relevance, and opportunities for frequent practice. Materials should include what students will read (reference books, fiction, poetry, expository text, newspaper articles, historic documents) and the technology they will use (Web sites, DVDs, CDs, word-processing programs, multimedia writing programs, instructional games, tutorials).

Teachers should obtain a range of fiction and nonfiction reading materials related to the topic that are appropriately leveled for multitiered reading instruction. Figure 6.1 shows examples of reading materials selected for the thematic unit about Africa. From the reading materials, teachers will identify relevant decoding skills and vocabulary words for direct instruction. Students will use these selected texts to practice fluency building (using partner reading, choral reading) and comprehension skills (such as identifying main ideas, making predictions, retelling). The thematic reading materials should also be connected with writing instruction. For example, students can write summaries, reactions, or opinions in response to reading passages. Students can also create their own stories or reports using the reading materials as models and sources of inspiration.

IDENTIFYING LANGUAGE-ARTS SKILLS

After materials are selected, teachers can make decisions about which language-arts skills to target. For example, in order to read and comprehend text, the students will need to learn specific vocabulary used in selected reading passages. Students must be able listen to pronunciation, definitions, and examples of vocabulary words; use the vocabulary word in context while speaking; pronounce and comprehend the vocabulary while reading; and write the vocabulary word correctly in context.

Peer editing is another example of a skill that provides an opportunity to logically connect the four levels of communication. For example, each student writes a paragraph and exchanges it with a peer. Each student then reads his or her peer's paragraph, makes edits, and writes feedback on a peer-editing form. After the reading and writing part of this activity is complete, the students can practice their speaking and listening skills by taking turns providing oral feedback to each other, listening to the feedback, and asking appropriate questions for clarification. After this discussion, the students will write their revisions, taking peer feedback into consideration. Figure 6.1 shows examples of connected listening, speaking, reading, and writing skills that can be used with any appropriate reading materials in a thematic unit (children's literature, content-area texts).

PLANNING MULTITIERED INSTRUCTION

Before planning instructional delivery, the selected theme should be divided into smaller units to make daily planning more manageable. Figure 6.1 shows the theme of Africa broken down into five parts. Social studies connections include geographical areas and sequential periods of history. Science connections include the study of wildlife and ecosystems in different geographic areas (jungle, grasslands, desert). The type of literature selected for this unit is folk tales that tell stories from different geographic regions of Africa (such as Liberia, Zimbabwe). Additionally, cultural arts (like sculpture and dance) are included in connection with social studies, science, and literature.

Instructional delivery of thematic units will include a combination of the following evidence-based practices: explicit instruction, active student responding, peer-mediated instruction, differentiated instruction, and extended time to practice connected language arts skills for authentic purposes (reading books, writing stories). The following section provides teachers with suggestions for planning instructional activities for multitiered instruction.

Introducing the thematic unit. When teaching a thematic unit, it is a good idea to introduce the unit and begin all of the lessons with an activity or event that will capture the students' interest and generate continued excitement about the theme. The opening activity or event should focus attention on the theme and connect the theme topic to the students' prior knowledge and experiences. The following are examples attention-getting activities:

- Open the lesson with interesting information or a question: "Where on the planet do you think human beings originated?"
- Hide an object related to the theme (like a toy dinosaur) from the students' view. Provide the students with hints and give them an opportunity to guess what it is.
- Open the lesson with a thought-provoking quote related to the theme: "It takes a village to raise a child." Then generate a discussion about its meaning.
- Begin the lesson with a song or a poem related to the unit (like "Abiyoyo" by Pete Seeger).
- Show pictures or videos related to the theme to prompt discussion.
- Use props or costumes to capture attention and stimulate discussion.
- Begin the lesson with a game or a movement activity (like dance) related to the unit.

The opening attention-getter should build student interest and lead to a discussion of the theme. Discussion should focus on how the theme is relevant to the students and how it relates to their background experiences. Teachers can then provide an overview of what the students will learn and the kinds of activities they can look forward to in the next few weeks.

Multitiered instruction. For each lesson, teachers should provide modeling, direct instruction, and guided practice of important concepts and skills to the whole class prior to having students work independently, in small, peer-mediated groups, or in more intensive arrangements. Guided practice activities that incorporate frequent active student responding will enable teachers to provide frequent feedback and monitor the extent to which students have mastered prerequisite skills. Well-executed guided practice activities will increase the likelihood of student success during independent tasks.

Additionally, teachers can increase motivation by providing students with choices. For example, the teacher can read the students a few different African proverbs (such as "Don't insult the crocodile until you cross the water;" "It is not what you are called, but what you answer to;" "You do not teach the paths of the forest to an old gorilla;" and "Rats don't dance in the cat's doorway."), and the students can select the one they want to write about.

For Tier 1 instruction, teachers should focus on decoding skills, vocabulary words, comprehension strategies, writing strategies, and any important concepts related to theme's content. Teachers can increase whole-class responding and immediate feedback for each response using choral responding, response cards, or guided notes. Following teacher-led guided practice activities, students can work in cooperative learning groups or peer tutoring dyads to practice basic reading skills, fluency building, or comprehension monitoring. Students can also work with a group, a peer, or independently on self-selected writing projects related to the theme.

Instruction in Tiers 2 and 3 can be implemented with small groups and individuals when many of the other students are working on independent assignments. The coteaching arrangements described in Chapter 1 (station teaching, alternative teaching) can also be used to provide more intensive instruction to the students who need it. For example, one teacher monitors the whole class while they are working on independent reading assignments while the other teacher works with small groups or individual students needing supplemental instruction. For literacy instruction in Tiers 2 and 3, teachers can provide additional instruction and drill with Tier 1 objectives (such as phonemic awareness, decoding, vocabulary words). Additionally, teachers can provide explicit instruction and guided practice using mnemonic strategies, graphic organizers, structured self-questioning strategies, or self-monitoring skills. Students receiving more intensive instruction can also use individualized computer programs to practice reading and writing skills. Figure 6.1 shows examples of multitiered instruction designed for Part 1 of the thematic unit on Africa. When planning for flexible multitiered instruction, teachers should use CBM progress monitoring and error analysis data to determine which students need more intensive instruction. Additionally, teachers can use performance-based assessment or rubrics (see Chapters 2 and 4) to evaluate thematic unit products such as written reports, narrative stories, or oral presentations.

Accommodations. When planning multitiered instruction, accommodations for diverse learners should be built into the overall plan. For this reason, teachers should identify on the planning sheet the kinds of accommodations students need. The following are examples of accommodations that students may need:

- Modified guided notes for students with writing fluency difficulties
- High-interest, low-vocabulary reading selections for students with limited vocabulary knowledge or limited English proficiency
- Tape-recorded reading passages for struggling readers
- Assistive technology (speech-to-text, text-to-speech, word prediction) for students with various reading and writing limitations
- Additional audio/visual materials for students with attention difficulties
- Content instruction with native language texts for English language learners
- Picture-based software programs for struggling readers and writers
- Self-management forms for motivation and organization
- Simplified directions for students with listening comprehension deficits
- Pencil grips for small motor coordination difficulties
- Slant boards for handwriting difficulties
- Frequent short breaks for students with attention difficulties
- Breaking down large assignments into manageable chunks for students with organization difficulties

These are just a few examples of different accommodations that can be used in an inclusive classroom. To determine appropriate accommodations for students with disabilities, teachers need to refer the student's Individual Education Program (IEP). To determine accommodations for a struggling learner who does not have an IEP, teachers must examine the student's needs and the demands of the environment (including curriculum, materials, instructional delivery) and figure out the least obtrusive ways to facilitate full participation. The school's intervention assistance team is also a good resource for problem solving to identify appropriate accommodations for individual students.

Enrichment. When designing instruction for thematic units, teachers should also be aware of the advanced learners who can benefit from participating in and/or leading enrichment activities. The following are examples of group and individual enrichment activities.

Have students do the following:

- Work together to plan and deliver a panel discussion or debate about a piece of literature or concept.
- Work as a group to research a topic and create a PowerPoint presentation to deliver to the class.
- Work in collaborative groups to write and act out short skits related to the theme.
- Write a public service announcement or commercial, videotape it, show it to the class, and lead a discussion.
- Use word-processing programs to create a historical newspaper (Alber, Martin, & Gammill, 2005)
- Research an author (major events, major works) and discuss how the author's personal experiences may have influenced his or her writing (Alber et al., 2005).
- Select a character in a story, justify the character's behaviors, write a defense of their actions, and support their position.

Well-designed thematic units can provide all students with enriching contexts for practicing language-arts skills and applying those skills to purposeful activities.

SUMMARY

Evidence-based practices for teaching literacy include integrating the four language arts and applying language-arts skills in meaningful contexts across the curriculum. One way to accomplish these objectives is to design multitiered literacy instruction within thematic units. When teachers combine their unique skills to collaboratively plan and implement thematic units, they can increase academic achievement and enthusiasm for learning. With thematic units, teachers can use the logical connections between reading and writing to improve instructional efficiency and increase generalized outcomes. The recursive steps for planning a thematic unit include selecting a theme, identifying goals, locating resources, planning multitiered learning activities, and determining the most appropriate assessments.

Consideration of the uniqueness of student backgrounds and abilities will enable teachers to design appropriate thematic units. The theme should grab the students' attention and inspire enthusiasm for learning. Theme categories may include curricular topics, current events, or literary interests. Once teachers decide upon a topic, they can use book webs or theme webs to begin organizing the theme. Instructional materials should be selected based upon student interests and reading levels. Multitiered instructional delivery of thematic units should provide balanced language-arts instruction that includes direct instruction, active student responding activities, peer-mediated instruction, and extended time to engage in purposeful reading and writing activities. When planning instruction, teachers should incorporate individual accommodations (such as modified guided notes, recorded reading passages) throughout the plan. Additionally, teachers should include a variety of challenging independent and small-group enrichment activities for students who are academically advanced or gifted.

7

Programming for Generalization of Literacy Skills

When teaching new skills, the goal is for students to attain mastery and use those skills independently in other appropriate places or situations, in different or creative ways, and over time (Cooper, Heron, & Heward, 2007). For example, generalization has occurred if a student, after learning to write his name on wide-ruled paper in the classroom, can also write his name at other locations, in different ways, using different kinds of paper and writing instruments, and throughout the school year. This example illustrates the three kinds of generalized outcomes described by Cooper and colleagues (2007): response maintenance, setting/situation generalization, and response generalization.

For a variety of reasons, some newly learned behaviors can continue for up to many years, while many other behaviors are only short lived. Response maintenance refers to the length of time a learner continues to perform a skill independently after instruction has been discontinued. For example, a first grader learned to decode 20 words with a consonant-vowel-consonant (CVC) pattern at the beginning of the school year and he can still decode them at the end of the school year. If he can also decode those words in different places with different reading materials, then setting/situation generalization has occurred. Setting/situation generalization is the extent to which new skills are performed independently in other settings or situations not directly taught. This type of generalization also occurs when students perform the target skill with different materials, different instructional arrangements, different peers, or at different times of the day.

Both setting/situation generalization and response maintenance require the learner to perform the skill in about the same way across settings and situations and over time. Response generalization, however, occurs when the student produces appropriate variations of the target behavior that have not been directly taught. Teachers can consider response generalization to be a form of creativity. For example, Ms. Calder demonstrates how using more action verbs can make written expression more interesting. She instructs her students to examine their stories and circle all of the uninteresting verbs like "was" and "went" and replace them with action verbs (like "stumbled," "fled," "bounced"). She provides the students with several practice examples in context and a list of action verbs to choose from during independent story-revision time. When one student, Cadee, revised her story, she used some of the action verbs on the teacher's list. Then she thought of different action verbs that were not directly taught and used them in her story too. Cadee's use of untaught action verbs in her story is an example of response generalization. Teachers should keep in mind that response generalization is not a desired outcome for every behavior. For many skills, there is only one correct answer and creative responding will only result in errors (as in spelling, phonetic rules, grammatical rules).

Evidence-based practices specifically designed to promote these three types of generalized outcomes have been identified in the applied behavior analysis literature (Osnes & Leiblein, 2003; Stokes & Baer, 1977). Based on decades of research, Cooper and colleagues (2007) identified the following five general strategies under which most generalization programming tactics can be categorized: (a) selecting representative teaching examples, (b) making the classroom resemble generalization settings, (c) providing students with a means to access reinforcement, (d) arranging ways to transfer the skill to different settings, and (e) training students to transfer skills. Teachers can program for generalized outcomes most effectively using a combination of these strategies. This chapter will describe how teachers can use each strategy to program for generalization of literacy skills.

SELECTING REPRESENTATIVE TEACHING EXAMPLES

This strategy refers to providing instruction and practice with examples that sample the range of possible situations the student is likely to encounter when performing the new skill. For example, when learning to locate definitions of words in the dictionary, students can practice this skill with several dictionaries differing in size, color, font, and number of pages.

Most teachers probably realize that in order for students to master a concept or skill, they need frequent practice with many different teaching examples. Thoughtful selection of a range of teaching examples will make instruction more efficient and effective. For example, when learning a decoding rule, teachers should provide examples that include a variety of words using the same rule. If students are learning to pronounce words with the C-V-C-e pattern, the teaching examples should include words with a range of previously taught vowel and consonant sounds (cake, rope, tune, dime). When students practice a range of examples, they are more likely to generalize the rule to new words that have the same pattern.

Developing the right examples also requires teachers to consider other aspects of the learning environment such as materials, method of instructional delivery, instructional arrangements (whole class, small group), and people delivering instruction (teacher, peer, paraprofessional). Listing and prioritizing the range of situations students will likely encounter will help teachers decide which examples to select for instruction. Taking into consideration mastery of prerequisite skills, the examples should be prioritized by how important they are and how frequently they are needed by the students (Cooper et al., 2007). The following are examples of this generalization strategy used for reading instruction:

- After students have learned many phonemes, have them practice recognizing and saying a range of different isolated sounds and initial, medial, and final sounds in words. Use different stimuli to prompt student responses such as pictures, real objects, books, songs, or poems. For example, the teacher can show students pictures and real objects (like a ball) and have them practice generating rhyming words.
- For decoding rules (short vowel sounds, syllabication, long vowel sounds), teach examples and nonexamples of the rule and have students practice applying the rule to many different words. When decoding words in context, teaching examples can include different structures of sentences and paragraphs, or stories of different lengths and genres.
- Students can practice oral reading fluency with different kinds of reading passages (such as narrative, expository), with and without pictures, with different-sized print, and using different procedures (including choral reading with a group, partner reading with a peer, independent reading with a tape recorder).
- For vocabulary, teachers should provide students with clear definitions that include many examples and nonexamples. Additionally, students should practice decoding, saying, and writing the new word in a wide range of different reading and conversational contexts.
- Students should practice reading comprehension skills with a range of different reading passages, reading stimuli (news articles, short stories, books, electronic files), and purposes (for enjoyment, to obtain information). Additionally, students can practice reading silently and aloud at different times and locations (such as the child's desk, a learning center in the classroom, school library, home).

Teachers must also select representative examples for the range of writing skills. Many revising and editing examples can be taught efficiently during the five-minute mini-lessons used in writer's workshop (Atwell, 1987). Use an overhead projector to model and demonstrate an editing skill (such as using quotation marks). When teaching students how to punctuate direct quotes, teaching examples should include direct quotes of statements ("I like this book," Steve said.), questions (Donna asked, "What is it about?"), and exclamations ("Ouch, you dropped it on my foot!"). Additionally, students need to learn how to punctuate direct quotations that occur at different places in a sentence ("Please help me," Linda said, "I lost my phone."). Check for understanding by calling on students to generate their own examples for the class to punctuate together. Generalization of each mini-lesson skill can be assessed by examining subsequent student writing.

Teachers can also teach representative examples for planning and organization of different types of writing (such as a news report, narrative story, persuasive paper, book review) using different kinds of graphic organizers (story maps, Venn diagrams). Additionally, teachers can show students reading passages that illustrate the different ways authors tell a story. For example, stories can be told in first or third person, from the perspectives of various characters or a detached narrator. Based on these models, students can practice different stylistic elements in their own writing.

MAKING THE CLASSROOM RESEMBLE GENERALIZATION SETTINGS

Two tactics for making the instructional setting (the classroom) similar to the generalization setting (the real world) are programming common stimuli and teaching loosely (Cooper et al., 2007).

Programming common stimuli. All reading and writing tasks have a lot in common (left-to-right orientation, standard letter and word spacing, spelling and grammar conventions). When teachers place emphasis on the common critical components of a skill during instruction, students are more likely to generalize the skill to other settings and situations. Programming common stimuli requires that teachers include common elements of the generalization setting into instruction. For example, almost all fiction stories everywhere have the same common elements (characters, setting, conflict, events, and resolution). In order to promote reading comprehension, Mr. Walker teaches the students to identify these common elements through the use of guided notes and story maps. He also provides guided and independent practice identifying critical story elements in context. Generalization is evident when the students are able to identify and comprehend these common elements in a range of new stories. Teachers can also program common stimuli of reading skills by teaching students a consistent rule or procedure for decoding words (like the DISSECT strategy), remembering vocabulary definitions (the Keyword method), summarizing text (paragraph shrinking), and monitoring comprehension (self-questioning).

For written expression, teachers can program common stimuli by teaching students a consistent way to approach, work through, and complete writing assignments. Teaching students the writing process approach is an example of programming common stimuli because this can be used for almost all writing genres (narrative, informative, expository, persuasive).

Mnemonic strategies for producing different kinds of written expression (such as C-SPACE for narrative writing and TOWER for expository writing) can also function as common stimuli that promote generalization. Students can also use mnemonic strategies to learn revising (SEARCH) and editing skills (COPS). See Table 5.1 for a list of mnemonic strategies that can be used as common stimuli for producing various types of written expression. Other examples of common stimuli that can be used to promote generalization across a range of writing assignments include word banks, dictionaries, thesauri, and checklists for revising and editing (see Chapter 5).

Teaching loosely. When students are learning to read and write, there are many aspects of the environment that should have little or no effect on their performance. Noncritical stimuli such as the color of the student's pencil, the location of the child's desk in the classroom, or the number of people in the classroom, should have no effect on the child's ability to execute a reading or writing task. However, noncritical stimuli often inhibit generalization for many students, especially those with disabilities. For example, prior to drafting a persuasive paper, students need to brainstorm arguments supporting an issue, consider opposing arguments, and organize their ideas from most to least compelling. Aspects of the writing environment such as the number of students in the room or the color of the bulletin boards should not affect a student's ability to write a persuasive paper. However, for many children, some noncritical stimuli may exert control over writing performance. A student may refuse to write on yellow paper because he is used to writing on white paper or a student may refuse to write in the morning because he is used to writing in the afternoon. Color of paper and time of day are two examples of noncritical stimuli that may take some control of writing behavior for some students. In order to prevent this problem, teachers should systematically vary noncritical stimuli of the environment (like noise level, lighting, aromas). Teachers can vary noncritical stimuli during both reading and writing instruction in the following ways:

- Provide reading and writing instruction using a variety of media. Teachers can deliver whole-class instruction using a chalkboard, dry-erase board, overhead projector, chart paper, interactive whiteboard, or LCD projector. Additionally, students can complete assignments using different word-processing programs, writing support programs (like speech to text, word prediction), or different kinds of paper and writing instruments.
- Allow students to read or write in different locations of the room and at different times of day. They can work alone at their desks, at a table with other students, or at a learning center. If students work with peers or a team, the teacher should also vary the peers with whom students are grouped.
- Vary the background noise by playing different kinds of music during independent reading or writing. Sometimes music can be selected to help inspire a writing task. For example, if the assignment is to write a poem that is rhythmically similar to Harlem Renaissance poetry, play jazz music from that era as background while students write.

PROVIDING STUDENTS WITH A MEANS TO ACCESS REINFORCEMENT

Five tactics that enable students to access reinforcement are: (a) teaching the student to perform a skill well enough to access reinforcement, (b) using "behavior traps" to motivate students, (c) asking significant others to notice and reinforce target skills, (d) teaching the student to recruit or request contingent reinforcement, and (e) programming unpredictable reinforcement (Cooper et al., 2007).

Teaching the student to perform a skill well enough to access reinforcement. The classroom has many powerful sources of reinforcement available to students. Examples include teacher attention (praise), tangible rewards (tokens), activity rewards (playing a game), and success (good grade, feeling of accomplishment). However, many students, especially those who have academic skill deficits, may not perform basic skills fluently enough to contact the reinforcement available in the regular classroom. For example, many students with disabilities can decode words accurately or spell words correctly, but if they read and write too slowly they may not be proficient enough to access available reinforcers. For this reason, teachers should include fluency training as part of reading and writing instruction. Fluency training consists of daily timed trials to increase proficiency of basic skills. To increase reading and writing proficiency, teachers can implement daily one- to three-minute timed trials for naming letters, reading sight words, reading words in context, writing spelling words, and writing continuous text. As students become more fluent with basic reading and writing skills, they will have more opportunities to contact natural reinforcement across a range of settings and situations.

Using "behavior traps" to motivate students. Another way to help students contact natural reinforcement for learning and practicing their literacy skills is using behavior traps. Baer and Wolf (1970) used the term "behavior trap" to describe a phenomenon in which powerful contingencies of reinforcement work almost automatically to produce generalized responding. For example, James, a sixth grader, is very interested in race cars. At home, he watches race cars on TV, plays race car video games, and researches race cars on the Internet. At school, he usually selects books about race car drivers during sustained silent reading time, and he often writes stories about race cars in his journal. For James, race cars are a behavior trap. Because race cars are a powerful reinforcer for James, his teacher uses this behavior trap to motivate James to maintain and extend his reading and writing skills. For example, she provides James with many different reading materials about race cars and encourages him to write different kinds of writing pieces about race cars. Many activities that are automatically reinforcing to students (such as playing video games, watching sports, listening to music) can easily be incorporated into reading and writing instruction. The best way to use behavior traps for teaching literacy is to help students find reading and writing topics that are personally meaningful (Alber-Morgan, Hessler, & Konrad, 2007).

Teachers can determine their students' interests by asking them what they like to do (collect unicorns, draw pictures, cook), where they like to go (baseball games, art galleries, the race track), and who their heroes are (pop stars, athletes, fictional characters). Teachers can also provide a variety of media and activities to sample and then observe students to determine if a special interest emerges. For reading, teachers can set behavior traps by allowing students to choose a high-interest topic and use the Internet to research the topic, select books to read about the topic, and work with peers on collaborative projects about the topic. Other examples of behavior traps for reading instruction include allowing students read and follow directions for a high-interest activity (like making paper airplanes or origami animals), reading song lyrics of a favorite musician, reading e-mails or notes from classmates, or reading comic books.

Teachers can use behavior traps in the following ways to program for generalized writing outcomes:

- Have the students interview a parent or grandparent to find out about their childhood memories, family legends, funny stories, and/or favorite recipes or remedies. Old photographs of family members can be used to inspire descriptive writing. Students can write a story or report of the interview to share with their classmates. Encouraging students to write about the unique and interesting aspects of their families and cultures will certainly be personally relevant.

- Use high-interest story starters to motivate student writing. Story starters can be pictures of people, places, and things for which the students have expressed an interest (ice skating, outer space, motorcycles). Story starters can also be a written or spoken sentence ("I suddenly woke up to a loud crashing sound."). Students can use the picture or sentence to generate ideas and write a story.

- Use favorite TV shows and actors to inspire students to write a screenplay or movie script for a favorite actor or series. Students can also write stories about or letters to their favorite pop stars or heroes.

- Read an excerpt from an action-packed book. Stop reading when you come to a cliffhanger and have students write what they think happens next.

- Have students cut out several pictures of characters from their favorite comic books or magazines (pop culture, fashion, music, sports) and paste them to poster board to form a story sequence. Then the students write what each character is saying in dialogue bubbles. This activity, which may be especially fun for reluctant writers, can launch into a more involved individual or collaborative writing piece.

- Have students who enjoy drawing write stories about their art work, create a comic strip, or make their own picture books. Using multimedia computer programs with graphics, animation, and sound effects can also be a behavior trap for writing.

- Have students write a "how to" paper about playing a favorite video game, cooking a favorite dish, playing a sport, or any other activity they enjoy doing.

Students are likely to see the connection between their written expression and positive consequences when they write for authentic purposes. Examples of writing that can produce natural reinforcement include writing a letter to a friend or family member, writing to a company to obtain free materials, writing to a fan club to obtain a signed photograph of a pop star, or writing an article or story for the class newspaper or Web site.

Asking significant others to notice and reinforce target skills. In order for a behavior to be emitted regularly in generalization settings outside the classroom, that behavior must contact reinforcement in those settings. The teacher cannot follow the student to all of the necessary generalization settings to reinforce reading and writing skills learned in the classroom. For this reason, teachers should ask significant others in the child's life to prompt and reinforce specific reading and writing skills. This will increase the likelihood that the student will transfer important literacy skills to other places outside the classroom. Significant others may include parents, siblings, extended family, other teachers, and paraprofessionals.

Teachers should regularly communicate with parents through conferences, telephone calls, e-mails, and notes. Through these communications, teachers can let parents know what skills their children are working on at school. Then they can ask parents to prompt and reinforce those skills at home. For example, students can take home self-selected books to read and discuss with family members. Parents can also make use of teachable moments by having students practice reading words they see in various locations throughout the day (such as the grocery store, dentist office, bank). Parents can take advantage of natural opportunities to write. For example, they can prompt and reinforce their children to write invitations, thank-you cards, shopping lists, captions for family photographs, or titles for drawings.

Teaching the student to recruit or request contingent reinforcement. Another way to contact reinforcement in the generalization setting is to ask for it. Although adult attention and approval are natural reinforcers available in most classrooms, desired behaviors can often go unnoticed and unreinforced. If desired behaviors are not reinforced, they are not likely to improve. In order to prevent this problem, students can be taught to tap into the natural contingency of reinforcement by recruiting teacher attention. For example, a child can be taught to raise his hand, wait for the teacher to call on him, and ask her to look at his work ("What do you think of this paragraph I wrote?"). This puts the child in control of accessing his own reinforcement (adult attention, feedback, praise). Teaching students to recruit reinforcement has been demonstrated to increase academic proficiency, positive social interactions, and generalized outcomes (Alber, Heward, & Hippler, 1999; Craft, Alber, & Heward, 1998). Students can even learn to recruit from peers during cooperative learning groups (Wolford, Heward, & Alber, 2001). Alber and Heward (1997) recommend the following guidelines for teaching student to recruit reinforcement:

- Teach students to check their work for completeness and accuracy before they recruit teacher attention.
- Use modeling and role-playing to teach students a simple recruiting sequence (raise your hand, wait for the teacher, ask your question in a polite voice, say thank you).
- Teach students to limit the number of times they recruit (one to three times per 20 minutes) to avoid becoming a pest.
- Give students a physical prompt and/or recording device for recruiting (an index card listing the recruiting steps, and a place on the card to record each recruiting response).

Programming unpredictable reinforcement. Another way to program for generalization using reinforcement is to make that reinforcement unpredictable. When teachers program for generalization, they prepare students for what to expect in the real world (outside the classroom). Contingencies of reinforcement in the real world are often intermittent, delayed, and unpredictable (Cooper et al., 2007). For example, speaking politely does not always result in getting your way, and working hard is not always followed by appreciative comments. Incorporating unpredictable schedules of reinforcement into reading and writing instruction can promote generalization by preparing students for the intermittent and delayed reinforcement contingencies operating outside the classroom.

Before implementing unpredictable schedules of reinforcement, teachers must first reinforce newly learned skills continuously (that is, after each response). This prevents students from practicing errors. After students reach a predetermined level of mastery, teachers can gradually thin the reinforcement to intermittent and delayed schedules. Initially, a teacher may provide praise and feedback after each complete sentence a student writes. Once the student demonstrates some proficiency with writing complete sentences, the teacher may move to an intermittent schedule by providing attention after an average of every two to four sentences. As students demonstrate increased writing proficiency, the teacher can provide them with delayed reinforcement. For example, if a student completes a writing assignment in the morning, he may get delayed reinforcement at the end of the school day (for example, a happy note to his parents). Teachers can use the following procedures to program unpredictable reinforcement of reading and writing skills:

- At the end of sustained silent reading (SSR), randomly select students to share something with the class about their reading selection.
- During reading or writing instruction, give tickets to students for correct answers, participation, and appropriate interactions. Have students write their names on the tickets for a prize drawing at the end of the week.
- Select a vocabulary word each day and give students tickets whenever they use that word correctly in context during speaking or writing tasks throughout the day.
- While students are engaged in independent reading or writing tasks, provide frequent and intermittent praise or tangible reinforcement (like stickers or tokens) for staying on task. Additionally, while students are working with peers, provide them with frequent and intermittent praise for their appropriate interactions (giving and receiving feedback).
- Regularly draw a few students' names out of a hat to determine who gets to read his or her story to the class. Students never know when they will be selected so many are likely to be ready when they are called.
- At the end of a writing period, randomly select one writing/editing skill that you will be assessing (such as capitalization, punctuation, subject-verb agreement, or complete sentences). Since students will not know which skill will be graded, they may be more likely to edit their work more carefully for many different skills. This can also save grading time.

ARRANGING WAYS TO TRANSFER SKILLS TO DIFFERENT SETTINGS

Mediating generalization is creating a means to transfer a skill from the learning setting to the generalization setting. Two ways to mediate generalization are contriving a transportable prompt and teaching self-management (Cooper et al., 2007).

Contrive a transportable prompt. A contrived prompt must help the student perform the target behavior, and it must be transportable from setting to setting (Baer, 1999). For example, the teacher can give students a laminated index card that lists the steps for using a particular writing strategy. The student can use that card as a reference tool for the writing strategy in the classroom. Additionally, the student can transport that card to other places where he needs to use that writing strategy (different classrooms, home, library). Other examples of transportable contrived mediating stimuli for reading and writing include pronunciation keys, dictionaries, story maps, self-questioning prompts, study guides, structured worksheets, and vocabulary lists.

Teach self-management. Students need to learn skills that will enable them to function with the greatest degree of independence possible. When students can set their own goals, and prompt, monitor, and reinforce their own behavior, then can generalize many different skills in a wide range of settings and situations. Students can self-manage their homework and daily assignments by writing them down and checking them off when they are completed. Students can also self-select reading goals and self-monitor the number of words, pages, or books they read using a recording form (see Figure 7.1).

The following are examples of ways to program for self-management of writing skills.

- Provide students with a writing folder or binder to keep all of their writing ideas and goals. Students can organize and sequence their ideas in order of what they find most interesting. They can self-select writing goals (such as a school news article, a play, an autobiography, an expository report) and create a timeline showing deadlines for each part of the more involved projects (pick a topic, gather information about the topic, organize the information, write a first draft). They can self-reinforce by checking off each part of the task completed and showing it to their teacher.
- Play tape-recorded intermittent tones and have the students self-record whether or not they are on task each time they hear a tone. Tactile prompts have also been demonstrated to be effective for self-monitoring of on-task behavior (Amato-Zech, Hoff, & Doepke, 2006). A pager-like device called a MotivAider can be clipped to the waistband and programmed to vibrate at fixed and intermittent intervals. Each time a child feels the brief vibration, he is prompted to self-record whether or not he is on task.
- Students can also self-monitor by counting and graphing the number of words they write during each class session or self-monitor the amount of time spent on writing outside of school.

Figure 7.1	Self-Monitoring Form for Reading

Name: _____			Goal _____ (pages)	
Book Title	**Date**	**Signature**	**Pages**	**Number of pages read**
			Total Pages _____	

TRAINING STUDENTS TO TRANSFER SKILLS

Two ways to train students to transfer skills include reinforcing novel responses and reminding the student to generalize (Cooper et al., 2007).

Reinforcing novel responses. Students can learn to be more creative when teachers reinforce their novel or creative responses. For example, teachers can praise students when they select unusual reading and research topics, create novel characters, use new vocabulary words in different contexts, or use novel metaphors. The best way to reinforce response variability for most students is through specific praise of creative responses. For example,

"*Meticulous*, good, I like how you used that interesting vocabulary word to describe your main character," or "Wow, that's an original idea for a story!" For some students it might be necessary to reinforce novel responses with tangible reinforcement (like stickers), but teachers should always pair the tangible reward with praise and specific feedback. Teachers can also encourage students to recognize and reinforce each other's creative responses (during peer editing).

Reminding the student to generalize. After teaching a new skill or strategy, teachers should remind the students to use the skill in other appropriate situations in and outside of the classroom. Teachers can discuss with students all of the various situations in which the students should use the new skill. For example, the teacher can say, "Now that you know how to use this summarizing strategy to help your reading comprehension, can you think of other times you should use this strategy?" Responses may include "in social studies class, in science class, when I'm doing my homework," and so on. The teacher can then instruct the student to use the strategy ("Now, when you read this chapter for homework tonight, make sure you use the summarizing strategy."). Teachers can also follow up by asking students to report other settings or situations where they used the strategy.

Reading and writing are challenging and complex language-arts skills that require proficiency with and synthesis of many component skills. Using the above activities to program for generalization, students will be able to experience the many ways reading and writing produce reinforcement. As students experience success across a range of situations, they are likely to extend their literacy skills to new and rewarding opportunities.

SUMMARY

The success of literacy instruction can be determined by the extent to which students can generalize and maintain skills learned in the classroom. Unless teachers explicitly program for generalization, students are unlikely to transfer newly learned skills to other settings, situations, behaviors, or over time. Teachers can use a combination of evidence-based strategies and tactics to program for setting/situation generalization, response generalization, and maintenance.

When teaching a new skill, teachers must select a representative range of teaching examples that enable students to transfer the skill to untaught examples. Teachers may also program for generalization by teaching students to focus on the common critical features of a task and to ignore aspects of the environment that are irrelevant to performing the skill. Providing students with a means to access reinforcement is a third strategy that includes teaching students to become more fluent, setting behavior traps, asking significant others to prompt and reinforce desired behaviors, teaching the student to recruit reinforcement, and making reinforcement unpredictable. Teachers can also contrive ways for students to perform target skills in other situations by providing transportable prompts, self-management strategies, and verbal reminders. Teachers can also teach students to be more creative by reinforcing their novel ideas.

8

Bridging the Research-to-Practice Gap

Two big disparities that have been pervasive in US education are the achievement gap and the research-to-practice gap. The achievement gap refers to the discrepancy of performance between high- and low-achieving students, and is correlated with disability, cultural and ethnic diversity, and income level (Casserly, 2006). The other gap, the research-to-practice gap, refers to an ongoing problem in which research-based teaching practices have had minimal, if any, carryover into real classrooms. Much to the detriment of our students, education has been driven more by fads than by the findings of scientific research (Kozloff, 2002). Recent federal legislation has attempted to bridge the achievement gap by also bridging the research-to-practice gap. Specifically, both NCLB (2002) and IDEIA (2004) require teachers to use instructional practices that are based on scientific research. Long before this legislation, the research-to-practice gap was a serious concern for teacher educators and researchers because applied research has not had much impact on actual practice (Cuban, 1993; Fuchs & Fuchs, 2001; Gersten, Morvant, & Brengelman, 1995).

To do their part in bridging the research-to-practice gap, teacher education programs must provide preservice teachers with an understanding of relevant evidence-based practices and authentic opportunities to apply those practices and evaluate the effects on student outcomes. Additionally, teacher preparation programs can enlighten preservice teachers to the value of consuming research and help them identify appropriate resources to independently obtain the information they need. After completing their university training, teachers may continue to have some exposure to evidence-based practices through staff development activities in the school districts where they are employed. These activities typically consist of lectures or workshops that may or may not be relevant or useful to individual teachers (Alber & Nelson, 2005). Additionally, insufficient follow up and support may be contributing factors to the overall ineffectiveness of traditional staff development (Fuchs & Fuchs, 2001; Joyce & Showers, 1995; Wood & Thompson, 1993).

Clearly, practicing teachers cannot rely on staff development alone to keep current with evidence-based practices. In order to select the best teaching practices for their students, teachers must be proactive in obtaining the information, resources, and experiences they need to become most effective. In addition to being consumers of research, teachers can also be producers and disseminators of research. The following are various ways to engage in professional development activities that will provide exposure to effective teaching practices that are supported by research.

CONSUMING RESEARCH

Joining a professional association devoted to the study of specific populations of students or content areas can provide teachers with access to a range of opportunities to learn about evidence-based teaching practices and how to best apply them in their own classrooms. Most teacher associations offer teachers access to research or practitioner journals, professional conferences, and many other teaching resources available on their Web sites. For example, the Council for Exceptional Children (CEC) offers Web seminars, audio files, regional workshops, and customized training. The following are examples of professional teacher associations, their Web sites, and journals. Additionally, Table 8.1 provides examples of a range of professional journals.

- Association for Direct Instruction (www.adihome.org/)
  Journal: *Journal of Direct Instruction*

- Council for Exceptional Children (www.cec.sped.org)
  Journals: *Exceptional Children, Teaching Exceptional Children*
  (Note: CEC also has 17 divisions, each with their own journals)

- International Reading Association (www.reading.org)
  Journals: *The Reading Teacher, Journal of Adolescent and Adult Literacy, Reading Research Quarterly*

- National Association for Bilingual Education (www.nabe.org/)
  Journal: *Bilingual Research Journal*

- National Association for the Education of Young Children (www.naeyc.org/)
  Journals: *Young Children, Teaching Young Children*

- National Association for Gifted Children (www.nagc.org)
  Journal: *Gifted Child Quarterly*

- National Council for the Social Studies (www.socialstudies.org)
  Journals: *Social Education, Social Studies and the Young Learner, Middle Level Learning*
- National Council of Teachers of English (www.ncte.org)
  Journals: *Language Arts, Voices From the Middle, English Journal*
- National Science Teachers Association (www.nsta.org/)
  Journals: *Science and Children, Science Scope, The Science Teacher*

Other Web sites where teachers can find resources for evidence-based teaching practices include the following: Center for Evidence-Based Practices (evidencebasedpractices.org), Intervention Central (www.intervention central.org), What Works Clearinghouse (ies.ed.gov/ncee/wwc/), Promising Practices Network (www.promisingpractices.net/programs.asp), Wing Institute (winginstitute.org), and the National Center for Special Education Research (ies.ed.gov/ncser). The US Department of Education (www.ed.gov/teachers) also provides teachers with classroom resources, materials, and lesson plans as well as opportunities for professional development.

Table 8.1 Examples of Research and Practitioner Journals

Assessment for Effective Intervention
Behavior Disorders
Behavioral Interventions
Bilingual Research Journal
Childhood Education
Education & Treatment of Children
Elementary School Journal
English Journal
Exceptional Children
Focus on Autism and Other Developmental Disabilities
Gifted Child Quarterly
Gifted Child Today
International Journal of Multicultural Education
Intervention in School and Clinic
Journal of Adolescent and Adult Literacy
Journal of Applied Behavior Analysis
Journal of Autism and Developmental Disorders
Journal of Behavioral Education
Journal of Communication Disorders
Journal of Direct Instruction
Journal of Education for Students Placed At Risk
Journal of Emotional and Behavioral Disorders

(Continued)

Table 8.1	(Continued)

Journal of Positive Behavior Interventions

Journal of Learning Disabilities

Journal of Science Education for Students with Disabilities

Journal of Secondary Gifted Education

Journal of Special Education

Language Arts

Learning Disabilities: Research & Practice

Learning Disability Quarterly

Middle Level Learning

Preventing School Failure

Reading and Writing Quarterly

Reading Research Quarterly

The Reading Teacher

Remedial and Special Education

Science and Children

The Science Teacher

Social Education

Social Studies and the Young Learner

Teaching Exceptional Children

Teaching Young Children

Voices from the Middle

Young Children

PRODUCING AND DISSEMINATING RESEARCH

In addition to being consumers of research, classroom teachers can also be producers and disseminators of research. They can collaborate with university researchers to become actively involved in designing interventions, collecting data, and reporting the results. Teachers can also be copresenters of their classroom research at professional conferences or coauthors of journal publications. Collaborative partnerships between practitioners and researchers have been recommended for bridging the research-to-practice gap in education (Alber & Nelson, 2002; Bondy & Brownell, 2004). Working with researchers to collect and analyze data can show teachers how they can act as agents of change for their own students. When teachers and researchers collaborate to produce research, they make decisions together about the intervention objectives, procedures, and materials based on the unique needs of a particular classroom. Teachers who are actively involved in classroom research will clearly see its relevance for their own students. Sharing the findings with other teachers is the next step in this process for bridging the research-to-practice gap.

Teachers can proactively seek out opportunities to become involved in classroom research by contacting their local university faculty to discuss their interests in conducting collaborative research in their own classrooms.

Graduate students who are working on thesis or dissertation research will typically need a real classroom for their data collection. When a teacher is involved in delivering systematic interventions and collecting data, the research has the potential to be more socially valid or acceptable to teachers. In addition to demonstrating positive effects for the students, collaborative classroom research may also demonstrate the feasibility and usability of an intervention that will encourage continued use.

Practicing teachers can also volunteer to mentor a student teacher and collaboratively design classroom research with the student teacher and university supervisor. Alber and Nelson (2005) describe step-by-step procedures for conducting collaborative classroom research with student and mentor teachers. First, the research team (mentor teacher, student teacher, university faculty, graduate student) must identify target students and their learning needs, develop research questions, determine possible interventions, define and decide how to measure the target behaviors, and select an appropriate experimental design and systematic procedures. Additionally, the research team must have regular meetings to analyze the data and make decisions about how to proceed. One of the most rewarding aspects of conducting classroom research is disseminating the findings to other teachers at school district workshops, at state conferences, at national and international conferences, and through publication in professional journals.

SUMMARY

The achievement gap and the research-to-practice gap have been common problems throughout the history of US education. Teachers can help bridge both of these gaps by proactively seeking out information and resources relevant to their own teaching situations. Teachers can be consumers of research by joining professional associations, reading professional journals, attending state and local conferences, and participating in relevant professional development activities offered by professional associations. In addition to being consumers of research, teachers can also make important contributions to the field by collaboratively presenting and publishing research.

References

Abbott, R. D., & Berninger, V. W. (1993). Structural equation modeling of relationships among developmental skills and writing skills in primary and intermediate grade writers. *Journal of Educational Psychology, 85,* 478–508.

Alber, S. R., & Foil, C. R. (2003). Drama activities that promote and extend your students' vocabulary proficiency. *Intervention in School and Clinic, 39,* 22–28.

Alber, S. R., & Heward, W. L. (1997). Recruit it or lose it! Training students to recruit positive teacher attention. *Intervention in School and Clinic, 32,* 275–282.

Alber, S. R., Heward, W. L., & Hippler, B. J. (1999). Teaching middle school students with learning disabilities to recruit positive teacher attention. *Exceptional Children, 65,* 253–270.

Alber, S. R., Martin, C. M., & Gammill, D. M. (2005). Using the literary masters to inspire gifted students' writing. *Gifted Child Today, 28,* 50–59.

Alber, S. R., & Nelson, J. S. (2002). Putting research in the collaborative hands of teachers and researchers: An alternative to traditional staff development. *Rural Special Education Quarterly, 21,* 24–32.

Alber, S. R., & Nelson, J. S. (2005). Collaborating with student and mentor teachers to design and implement classroom research. In W. L. Heward, T. E. Heron, N. A. Neef, S. M. Peterson, D. M. Sainato, G. Cartledge, et al. (Eds.), *Focus on Behavior Analysis in Education: Achievements, Challenges, & Opportunities* (pp. 173–187). Upper Saddle River, NJ: Merrill/Prentice Hall.

Alber, S. R., Nelson, J. S., & Brennan, K. B. (2002). A comparative analysis of two homework study methods on elementary and secondary students' acquisition and maintenance of social studies content. *Education and Treatment of Children, 25,* 172–196.

Alber-Morgan, S. R., Hessler, T., & Konrad, M. (2007). Teaching writing for keeps. *Education and Treatment of Children, 30,* 107–128.

Alber-Morgan, S. R., Ramp, E. M., Anderson, L. L., & Martin, C. M. (2007). The effects of repeated readings, error correction, and performance feedback on the fluency and comprehension of middle school students with behavior problems. *Journal of Special Education, 41,* 17–30.

Allison, B. N., & Rhem, M. L. (2007). Effective teaching strategies for middle school learners in multicultural, multilingual classrooms. *Middle School Journal, 39,* 12–18.

Amato-Zech, N., Hoff, K., & Doepke, K. (2006). Increasing on-task behavior in the classroom: Extension of self-monitoring strategies. *Psychology in the Schools, 43,* 211–221.

Anders, P. L., & Bos, C. S. (1986). Semantic feature analysis: An interactive strategy for vocabulary development text comprehension. *Journal of Reading, 29,* 610–617.

Anderson, C. L., & Anderson, K. M. (2006). Applying backward design principles to planning an inclusive thematic unit on China. *Special Education Technology Practice, 9,* 18–25.

Anderson, P. L. & Corbet, L. (2008). Literature circles for students with learning disabilities. *Intervention in School and Clinic, 4*, 25–33.

Aronson, E., Blaney, N., Stephin, C., Sikes, J., &. Snapp, M. (1978). *The jigsaw classroom.* Beverly Hills, CA: Sage.

Atkinson, R. C. (1975). Mnemotechnics in second-language learning. *American Psychologist, 30*, 821–828.

Atwell, N. (1987). *In the middle: Writing, reading, and learning with adolescents.* Portsmouth, NH: Heinemann.

Baer, D. M. (1999). *How to plan for generalization.* Austin, TX: PRO-ED.

Baer, D. M., & Wolf, M. M. (1970). The entry into natural communities of reinforcement. In R. Ulrich, T. Stachnik, & J. Mabry (Eds.), *Control of human behavior* (Vol. 2, pp. 319–324). Glenview, IL: Scott Foresman.

Baker, S., Gersten, R., & Graham, S. (2003). Teaching expressive writing to students with learning disabilities: Research-based applications and examples. *Journal of Learning Disabilities, 36*, 109–123.

Barrentine, S. J. (1999). Facilitating preservice students' development of thematic units. *The Teacher Educator, 34*, 276–290.

Blume, J. (1972). Tales of a fourth grade nothing. New York: Puffin Books.

Bolak, K., Bialach, D., & Dunphy, M. (2005). Standards-based, thematic units integrate the arts and energize students and teachers. *Middle School Journal, 36*, 9–19.

Bondy, E., & Brownell, M. T. (2004). Getting beyond the research to practice gap: Researching against the grain. *Teacher Education and Special Education, 27*, 47–56.

Brown-Chidsey, R., & Steege, M. W. (2005). *Response to intervention: Principles and strategies for effective practice.* New York: Guilford.

Bursuck, W. D., & Damer, M. (2007). *Reading instruction for students who are at risk or who have disabilities.* Boston: Pearson.

Busch, T. W., & Espin, C. A. (2003). Using curriculum-based measurement to prevent failure and assess learning in the content areas. *Assessment for Effective Intervention, 28*, 49–58.

Carle, E. (2004). *Mister Seahorse.* New York: Philomel Books.

Carnine, D. W., Silbert, J., Kame'enui, E. J., & Tarver, S. (2004). *Direct instruction reading* (4th ed.). Upper Saddle River, NJ: Prentice Hall.

Casserly, M. (2006). *Beating the odds: A city-by-city analysis of student performance and achievement gaps on state assessments: Results from the 2004–2005 school year.* Washington, DC: Council of Great City Schools.

Center for Applied Special Technology. (2007, November 8). *Summary of 2007 national summit on universal design for learning working groups.* (Report prepared for summit participants). Wakefield, MA.

Coker, D. (2006). Impact of first-grade factors on the growth and outcomes of urban schoolchildren's primary-grade writing. *Journal of Educational Psychology, 98*, 471–488.

Cole, C. M., Waldron, N., & Majd, M. (2004). Academic progress of students across inclusive and traditional settings. *Mental Retardation, 42*, 136–144.

Conner, D. J., & Ferri, B. A. (2007). The conflict within: Resistance to inclusion and other paradoxes in special education. *Disability and Society, 22*, 63–77.

Cooper, J. O., Heron, T. E., & Heward, W. L. (2007) *Applied behavior analysis* (2nd ed.) Upper Saddle River, NJ: Merrill/Prentice Hall.

Cooter, R. B., Jr., Flynt, E. S., & Cooter, K. S. (2007). *Comprehensive reading inventory: Measuring reading development in regular and special education classrooms.* Upper Saddle River, NJ: Pearson Education.

Craft, M. A., Alber, S. R., & Heward, W. L. (1998). Training elementary students with developmental disabilities to recruit teacher attention in a general education classroom: Effects on teacher praise and academic productivity. *Journal of Applied Behavior Analysis, 31*, 399–415.

Craig, J., Butler, A., Cairo, L., III, Wood, C., Gilchrist, C., Holloway, J., Williams, S., & Moats, S. (2005). *A case study of six high-performing schools in Tennessee.* Charleston, WV: Edvantia.

Crandall, J. A., Jaramillo, A., Olsen, L., & Peyton, J. K. (2001). Diverse teaching strategies for immigrant children. In R. W. Cole (Ed.), *More strategies for educating everybody's children* (pp. 33–71). Alexandria, VA: Association for Supervision and Curriculum Development.

Cuban, L. (1993). The lure of curricular reform and its pitiful history. *Phi Delta Kappan, 75,* 182–185.

Cusumono, D. L. (2007). Is it working?: An overview of curriculum-based measurement and its uses for assessing instructional, intervention, or program effectiveness. *The Behavior Analyst Today, 8,* 24–34.

Dalton, B., Sable, J., & Hoffman, L. (2006). *Characteristics of the 100 largest public elementary and secondary school districts in the United States: 2003–2004.* Washington, DC: National Center for Educational Statistics.

De La Paz, S., & Graham, S. (1997). Strategy instruction in planning: Effects on the writing performance and behavior of students with learning difficulties. *Exceptional Children, 63,* 167–181.

Deno, S. L. (2003). Developments in curriculum-based measurement. *Journal of Special Education, 37,* 184–192.

DiSpirt, D. (2008). Strategies to summarize a narrative: Teaching the main ideas or events in a story. *Suite 101.com.* Retrieved December 17, 2009, from http:// primary-school-lesson-plans.suite101.com/

Edelen-Smith, P. J. (1997). How now brown cow: Phoneme awareness activities for collaborative classrooms. *Intervention in School and Clinic, 33,* 103–111.

Ellis, E. S., & Friend, P. (1991). Adolescents with learning disabilities. In B. Y. L. Wong (Ed.), *Learning about learning disabilities* (pp. 505–561). San Diego: Academic Press.

Engelmann, S., & Carnine, D. W. (1982). *Theory of instruction: Principles and applications.* New York: Irvington.

Engelmann, S., & Silbert, J. (1983). *Expressive writing 1.* Chicago: Science Research Associates

Espin, C. A., De La Paz, S., Scierka, B. J., & Roelofs, L. (2005). The relationship between curriculum-based measures in written expression and quality and completeness of expository writing for middle school students. *Journal of Special Education, 38,* 208–217.

Espin, C. A., Scierka, B. J., Skare, S., & Halverson, N. (1999). Curriculum-based measures in writing for secondary students. *Reading and Writing Quarterly, 15,* 5–28.

Espin, C. A., Shin, J., Deno, S. L., Skare, S., Robinson, S., & Benner, B. (2000). Identifying indicators of written expression proficiency for middle school students. *Journal of Special Education, 34,* 140–153.

Espin, C. A., Wallace, T., Campbell, H., Lembke, E. S., Long, J. D., & Ticha, R. (2008). Curriculum-based measurement in writing: Predicting the success of high-school students on state standards tests. *Exceptional Children, 74,* 174–193.

Fairfax County Public Schools. (2004). *PALS: Performance assessment for language students.* Retrieved December 17, 2009, from http://www.fcps.edu/DIS/OHSICS/forlang/PALS/rubrics/

Fass, S., & Cauthen, N. K. (2008). *Who are America's poor children?* New York: National Center for Children in Poverty.

Ferguson, C. (2002). Using the revised taxonomy to plan and deliver team-taught, integrated, thematic units. *Theory to Practice, 41,* 238–243.

Flynt, E. S., & Cooter, R. B. (1999). *English-Español reading inventory for the classroom.* Upper Saddle River, NJ: Merrill.

Foil, C. R., & Alber, S. R. (2002). Fun and effective ways to build your students' vocabulary. *Intervention in School and Clinic, 37,* 131–139.

Foorman, B. R., Schatschneider, C., Eakin, M. N., Fletcher, J. M., Moats, L. C., & Francis, D. J. (2006). The impact of instructional practices in grades 1 and 2 on reading and spelling achievement in high-poverty schools. *Contemporary Educational Psychology, 31,* 1–29.

Friend, M., & Bursuck, W. D. (2009). *Including students with special needs: A practical guide for classroom teachers* (5th ed.). Upper Saddle River, NJ: Pearson.

Fuchs, D., & Fuchs, L. S. (2001). One blueprint for bridging the gap: Project PROMISE. *Teacher Education and Special Education, 24,* 304–314.

Fuchs, D., & Fuchs, L. S. (2004). Determining adequate yearly progress from kindergarten through grade 6 with curriculum-based measurement. *Assessment for Effective Instruction, 29,* 25–37.

Fuchs, D., & Fuchs, L. S. (2006). New directions in research: Introduction to response to intervention: What, why, and how valid is it? *Reading Research Quarterly, 41,* 93–99.

Fuchs, L. S., & Fuchs, D. (2007). Progress monitoring within a multi-tiered prevention system. *Perspectives on Language and Literacy, 33,* 43–47.

Fuchs, L. S., Fuchs, D., Hamlet, C. L., Waltz, L., & Gernmann, G. (1993). Formative evaluation of academic progress: How much growth can we expect? *School Psychology Review, 22,* 27–49.

Fuchs, D., Fuchs, L. S., & Vaughn, S. (2008). *Response to intervention.* Newark, DE: International Reading Association.

Gersten, R., Baker, S. K., Shanahan, T., Linan-Thompson, S., Collins, P., & Scarcella, R. (2007). *Effective literacy and English language instruction for English learners in the elementary grades: A practice guide* (NCEE 2007-4011). Washington, DC: National Center for Education Evaluation and Regional Assistance, Institute of Education Sciences, US Department of Education.

Gersten, R., Compton, D., Connor, C. M., Dimino, J., Santoro, L., Linan-Thompson, S. et al. (2009). *Assisting students struggling with reading: Response to intervention and multitier intervention for reading in the primary grades. A practice guide.* (NCEE 2009-4045). Washington, DC: National Center for Education Evaluation and Regional Assistance, Institute of Education Sciences, US Department of Education.

Gersten, R., Morvant, M., & Brengelman, S. (1995). Close to the classroom is close to the bone: Coaching as a means to translate research into practice. *Exceptional Children, 62,* 56–67.

Gillingham, A., & Stillman, B. W. (1970). *Remedial training for children with specific disability in reading, spelling, and penmanship.* Cambridge, MA: Educators Publishing Service.

Goldberg, A., Russell, M., & Cook, A. (2003). The effect of computers on student writing: A meta-analysis of studies from 1992–2002. *Journal of Technology, Learning, and Assessment, 2,* 1–51.

Good, R. H., III, Simmons, D. C., & Kame'enui, E. J. (2001). The importance and decision-making utility of a continuum of fluency-based indicators of foundational reading skills for third grade high-stakes outcomes. *Scientific Studies of Reading, 5,* 257–288.

Graham, S. (1983). The effect of self-instructional procedures on LD students' handwriting performance, *Learning Disability Quarterly, 6,* 231–234.

Graham, S. (1997). Executive control in the revising of students with learning and writing difficulties. *Journal of Educational Psychology, 89,* 223–234.

Graham, S., & Harris, K. R. (1989). Improving learning disabled students' skills at composing essays: Self-instructional strategy training. *Exceptional Children, 56,* 201–214.

Graham, S., & Harris, K. R. (1992). Cognitive strategy instruction in written language for learning disabled students. In S. Vogel (Ed.), *Educational alternatives for students with learning disabilities* (pp. 95–115). New York: Springer Verlag.

Graham, S., & Harris, K. R. (2003). Students with learning disabilities and the process of writing: A meta-analysis of SRSD studies. In L. Swanson, K. R. Harris, &

S. Graham (Eds.), *Handbook of research on learning disabilities* (pp. 323–344). New York: Guilford.

Graham, S., & Harris, K. R. (2005). *Writing better: Teaching writing processes and self-regulation to students with learning difficulties.* Baltimore: Brookes.

Graham, S., Harris, K. R., & Fink, B. (2000). Extra handwriting instruction: Prevent writing difficulties right from the start. *Teaching Exceptional Children, 33,* 88–91.

Graham, S., Harris, K. R., & Loynachan, C. (1993). The basic spelling vocabulary list. *Journal of Educational Research, 86,* 363–369.

Graham, S., & Miller, L. (1979). Spelling research and practice: A unified approach. *Focus on Exceptional Children, 12,* 1–6.

Graham, S., Olinghouse, N. G., & Harris, K. R. (2009). Teaching composing to students with learning disabilities: Scientifically supported recommendations. In G. A. Troia (Ed.), *Instruction and assessment for struggling writers: Evidence-based practices* (pp. 165–186). New York: Guildford.

Graham, S., & Perin, D. (2007). *Writing next: Effective strategies to improve writing of adolescents in middle and high school.* Washington, DC: Alliance for Excellence in Education.

Graves, D. H. (1994). *A fresh look at writing.* Portsmouth, NH: Heinemann.

Graves, D. H., & Rueda, R. (2009). Teaching written expression to culturally and linguistically diverse learners. In G. A. Troia (Ed.), *Instruction and assessment for struggling writers: Evidence-based practices* (pp. 213–242). New York: Guildford Press.

Greenwood, C. R., Delquadri, J. D., Hou, S., Terry, B., Arreaga-Mayer, C., & Abbott, M. (2001). *Together we can! Classwide peer tutoring learning management system teacher's manual.* University of Kansas: Sopris West.

Hagin, R. A. (1983). Write right—or left: A practical approach to handwriting. *Journal of Learning Disabilities, 16,* 266–271.

Hand, B., Hohenshell, L., & Prain, V. (2004). Exploring students' responses to conceptual questions when engaged with planned writing experiences: A study with year ten science students. *Journal of Research in Science Teaching, 41,* 186–210.

Hanover, S. (1983). Handwriting comes naturally? *Academic Therapy, 18,* 407–412.

Heron, T. E., Okyere, B. A., & Miller, A. D. (1991). A taxonomy of approaches to teach spelling. *Journal of Behavioral Education, 1,* 117–130.

Hessler, T., & Konrad, M. (2008). Using curriculum-based measurement to drive IEPs and instruction in written expression. *Teaching Exceptional Children, 41,* 28–37.

Heward, W. L. (1994). Three "low-tech" strategies for increasing the frequency of active student response during group instruction. In R. Gardner, D. Sainato, J. Cooper, T. Heron, W. Heward, J. Eshleman, et al. *Behavior Analysis in Education: Focus on measurably superior instruction* (pp. 283–320). Upper Saddle River, NJ: Prentice Hall.

Hopstock, P., & Stephenson, S., (2003). *Native languages of limited English proficient students.* Washington, DC: US Department of Education.

Horn, E. (1954). Phonics and spelling. *Journal of Education, 136,* 233–246.

Hosp, M. K., Hosp, J. L., & Howell, K. W. (2007). *The ABCs of CBM: A practical guide to curriculum-based measurement.* New York: Guilford Press.

Individuals with Disabilities Education Improvement Act. (2004). *Public Law No. 108-446.* Retrieved December 11, 2009, from http://www.copyright.gov/legislation/pl108-446.pdf

Idol, L. (2006). Toward the inclusion of special education students in general education: A program of evaluation in eight schools. *Remedial and Special Education, 27,* 77–94.

Jochum, J., Curran, C., & Reetz, L. (1998). Creating individual educational portfolios in written language. *Reading and Writing Quarterly, 14, 283–306.*

Johns, J. L. (2005). *Basic reading inventory* (9th ed.). Dubuque, IA: Kendall/Hunt.

Joyce, B., & Showers, B. (1995). *Student achievement through staff development* (2nd ed.). White Plains, NY: Longman.

Kamil, M. L., Borman, G. D., Dole, J., Kral, C. C., Salinger, T., & Torgesen, J. (2008). *Improving adolescent literacy: Effective classroom and intervention practices: A Practice Guide* (NCEE #2008-4027). Washington, DC: National Center for Education Evaluation and Regional Assistance, Institute of Education Sciences, US Department of Education.

Kamps, D. M., & Greenwood, C. R. (2005). Formulating secondary-level reading interventions. *Journal of Learning Disabilities, 38,* 500–509.

King-Sears, M. E., Mercer, C. D., & Sindelar, P. (1992). Toward independence with keyword mnemonics: A strategy for science vocabulary instruction. *Remedial and Special Education, 13,* 22–33.

Korinek, L., & Bulls, J. A. (1996). SCORE A: A student research paper writing strategy. *Teaching Exceptional Children, 28,* 60–63.

Kozloff, M. A. (2002) *Fad, Fraud, and Folly in Education,* Watson School of Education, University of North Carolina at Wilmington. Retrieved December 18, 2009, from http://people.uncw.edu/kozloffm/fads.html

Leaf, M. (1936). *Ferdinand.* New York: Viking Press.

Lenz, B. K., Schumaker, J. B., Deshler, D. D., & Beals, V. L. (1984). *Learning strategies curriculum: The word-identification strategy.* Lawrence, KS: University of Kansas.

Levin, J. R. (1988). Elaboration-based learning strategies: Powerful theory—powerful application. *Contemporary Educational Psychology, 13,* 191–205.

MacArthur, C. A. (1996). Using technology to enhance the writing processes of students with learning disabilities. *Journal of Learning Disabilities, 29,* 344–354.

MacArthur, C. A. (2009). Using technology to teach composing to struggling writers. In G. A. Troia (Ed.), *Instruction and assessment for struggling writers: Evidence-based practices* (pp. 243–268). New York: Guilford.

MacArthur, C. A., Graham, S., Schwartz, S. S., & Schafer, W. D. (1995). Evaluation of a writing instruction model that integrated a process approach, strategy instruction, and word processing. *Learning Disability Quarterly, 18,* 278–291.

Maheady, L., Harper, G. F., & Mallette, B. (2001). Peer-mediated instruction and interventions and students with mild disabilities. *Remedial and Special Education, 22,* 4–14.

Marchisan, M., & Alber, S. R. (2001). The write way: Tips for teaching the writing process to resistant writers. *Intervention in School and Clinic, 36,* 154–162.

Mason, L. H. & Graham, S. (2008). Writing instruction for adolescents with learning disabilities: Programs of intervention research. *Learning Disabilities Research & Practice, 23,* 103–112.

Mastropieri, M. A., & Scruggs, T. E. (1998). Enhancing school success with mnemonic strategies. *Intervention in School and Clinic, 33,* 201–208.

Mastropieri, M. A., Scruggs, T. E., & Fulk, B. J. M. (1990). Teaching abstract vocabulary with the keyword method: Effects on recall and comprehension. *Journal of Learning Disabilities, 23,* 293–296.

McGlinchey, M. T., & Hixson, M. D. (2004). Using curriculum based measurement to predict performance on state assessments in reading. *School Psychology Review, 33,* 193–203.

McKenna, M. C., Labbo, L. D., Reinking, D., & Zucker, T. A. (2007). Effective use of technology in literacy instruction. In L. B. Gambrell, L. M. Morrow, & M. Pressley (Eds.), *Best practices in literacy instruction* (pp. 334–372). New York: Guilford.

McKenna, M. C., & Stahl, K. A. D. (2009). *Assessment for reading instruction* (2nd ed.). New York: Guildford.

McLesky, J. (2004). Classic articles in special education. *Remedial and Special Education, 25,* 79–87.

McLesky, J., & Waldron, N. L. (2007). Comprehensive school reform and inclusive schools, *Theory Into Practice, 45,* 269–278.

McMaster, K. L., Fuchs, D., & Fuchs, L. S. (2006). Research on peer-assisted learning strategies: The promise and limitations of peer-mediated instruction. *Reading and Writing Quarterly, 22*, 5–25.

McQuiston, K., O'Shea, D., & McCollin, M. (2008). Improving phonological awareness and decoding skills of high school students from diverse backgrounds. *Preventing School Failure, 52*, 67–70.

Meinbach, A. M., Fredericks, A., & Rothlein, L. (2000). *The complete guide to thematic units: Creating the integrated curriculum* (2nd ed.). Norwood, MA: Christopher-Gorden.

Morrow, L. M., Pressley, M., Smith, J. K., & Smith, M. S. (1997). The effects of a literature-based program integrated into literacy and science instruction with children from diverse backgrounds. *Reading Research Quarterly, 32*, 54–76.

Mueller, J. (2008). *Authentic assessment toolbox.* Retrieved December 18, 2009, from http://jonathan.mueller.faculty.noctrl.edu/toolbox/howstep4.htm

National Association for Gifted Children. (2008). *Frequently asked questions.* Retrieved July 15, 2009, from http://www.nagc.org/index2.aspx?id=548.

National Association for the Education of Homeless Children and Youth. (2009). *Funding for the education for homeless children and youth program* (FY2010 appropriations). Retrieved August 22, 2009, from http://www.naehcy.org/update.html

National Center for Education Statistics. (2007). *2007 Reading Assessment.* Washington, DC: US Department of Education

National Center for Education Statistics. (2007a). *Contexts of elementary and secondary education.* Retrieved June 12, 2009, from http://nces.ed.gov/programs/coe/2007/section4/table.asp?tableID=717.

National Reading Panel. (2000). *Teaching children to read: An evidence-based assessment of the scientific research literature on reading and its implications for reading instruction* (National Institute of Health Pub. No. 00-4769). Washington, DC: National Institute of Child Health and Human Development.

National Symposium on Learning Disabilities in English Language Learners. (2004). *Symposium Summary.* Washington, DC: US Department of Special Education and Rehabilitation Services.

North Central Regional Educational Laboratory. (2005). *Implementing the No Child Left Behind Act: Teacher quality improves student achievement.* Naperville, IL: Learning Point Associates.

Office of English Language Acquisition, Language Enhancement, and Academic Achievement for Limited English Proficient Students (2008). *Biennial report to congress on the implementation of the Title III state formula grant program, school years 2004–06.* Washington, DC: U.S. Department of Education.

Ohio Department of Education. (2009) *Academic Content Standards.* Retrieved December 20, 2009, from http://ims.ode.state.oh.us/ODE/IMS/ACS

Okyere, B. A., Heron, T. E., & Goddard, Y. (1997). Effects of self-correction on the acquisition, maintenance, and generalization of the written spelling of elementary school children. *Journal of Behavioral Education, 7*, 51–69.

Osnes, P. G. & Lieblein, T. (2003). An explicit technology of generalization, *The Behavior Analyst Today, 3*, 364–374.

Persky, H. R., Daane, M. C., & Jin, Y. (2003). *The nation's report card: Writing 2002,* NCES 2003-529, Institute of Education Sciences. National Center for Education Statistics. Washington, DC: US Department of Education.

Pierce, L. V. & O'Malley, J. M. (1992). *Performance and portfolio assessment for language minority students.* Washington, DC: National Clearinghouse for Bilingual Education.

Powell-Smith, K. A., & Shinn, M. R. (2004). *Administration and scoring of written expression curriculum-based measurement for use in general outcome measurement.* Eden Prairie, MN: Edformation.

Ramirez, R. D., & Shapiro, D. S. (2007). Cross-language relationship between Spanish and English language learners in bilingual education classrooms. *Psychology in the Schools, 44,* 795–806.

Randolph, J. J. (2007). Meta-analysis of the research on response cards: Effects on test achievement, quiz achievement, participation, and off-task behavior. *Journal of Positive Behavioral Interventions, 9,* 113–128.

Reis, E. M. (1989). Activities for improving the handwriting skills of learning-disabled students. *The Clearing House, 62,* 217–219.

Rhoder, C. (2002). Mindful reading: Strategy training that facilitates transfer. *Journal of Adolescent & Adult Literacy, 45,* 498–512.

Robinson, F. R. (1970) *Effective study* (4th ed.). New York: Harper & Row.

Santangelo, T., & Quint, W. (2008). Planning and text production difficulties commonly experienced by students with learning disabilities: A synthesis of research to inform instruction. *Insights on Learning Disabilities 5,* 1–10.

Schirmer, B. R. & Bailey, J. (2000). Writing assessment rubric. *Teaching Exceptional Children, 33*(1), 52–58.

Schlagel, B. (2007). Best practices in spelling and handwriting. In S. Graham, C. A. MacArthur, & J. Fitzgerald (Eds.), *Best practices in writing instruction.* New York: Guilford.

Schoolfield, L. D., & Timberlake, J. B. (1960). *The phonovisual method.* Washington, DC: Phonovisual Products.

Schumaker, J. B. (2003). The theme writing strategy: Instructor's manual. Lawrence, KS: University of Kansas Institute for Research in Learning Disabilities.

Schumaker, J. B., Nolan, S. N., & Deschler, D. D. (1985). *Learning strategies curriculum: The error monitoring strategy.* Lawrence, KS: University of Kansas.

Shanahan, T. (2009). Connecting reading and writing instruction for struggling learners. In G. A. Troia (Ed.), *Instruction and assessment for struggling writers: Evidence-based practices* (pp. 113–131). New York: Guildford.

Shinn, M. M., & Shinn, N. R. (2002). *AIMSweb® training workbook.* Eden Prairie, MN: Edformation.

Silverstein, S. (1974). *Where the sidewalk ends.* New York: Harper and Row.

Snowman, J., & Biehler, R. (2003). *Psychology applied to teaching* (10th ed.). Boston: Houghton Mifflin.

Spinelli, C. G. (2008). Addressing the issue of cultural and linguistic diversity and assessment: Informal evaluation measures for English language learners. *Reading & Writing Quarterly, 24,* 101–118.

Stevens, R. J. (2006). Integrated reading and language arts instruction. *Research in Middle Level Education Online, 30,* 1–12. Retrieved December 20, 2009, from http://www.nmsa.org/Publications/RMLEOnline/tabid/426/Default.aspx.

Stokes, T. F., & Baer, D. M. (1977). An implicit technology of generalization. *Journal of Applied Behavior Analysis, 10,* 349–367.

Sturm, J. M., Rankin, J. L., Beukelman, D. R., & Schultz-Muehling, L. (1997). How to select appropriate software for computer-assisted writing. *Intervention in School and Clinic, 32,* 148–161.

Swicegood, P. (1994). Portfolio-based assessment practices. *Intervention in School and Clinic, 30,* 6–16.

Taba, H. (1967). *Teacher's handbook for elementary social studies.* Reading, MA: Addison-Wesley.

Taylor, L. K., Alber, S. R., & Walker, D. W. (2002). A comparative analysis of a modified self-questioning strategy and story mapping on the reading comprehension of elementary students with learning disabilities. *Journal of Behavioral Education, 11,* 69–87.

Thames, D. G., Reeves, C., Kazelskis, R., York, K. Boling, C., Newell, K., et al. (2008). Reading comprehension: Effects of individualized, integrated language arts as a reading approach with struggling readers. *Reading Psychology, 29,* 86–115.

Troia, G. A., Lin, S. C., Monroe, B. W., & Cohen, S. (2009). The effects of writing workshop instruction on the performance and motivation of good and poor writers In G. A. Troia (Ed.), *Instruction and assessment for struggling writers: Evidence-based practices* (pp. 77–112). New York: Guilford.

United Nations Educational, Scientific, and Cultural Organization. (2004). *The plurality of literacy and its implications for policies and programs.* (Position Paper). Paris: United National Educational, Scientific and Cultural Organization.

US Department of Education. (2007). *Individuals with disabilities education act (IDEA) data.* Washington, DC: US Government Printing Office.

US Department of Education. (2002). *No Child Left Behind: A desktop reference.* Washington, DC: Education Publications Center.

Vaughn, S., Bos, C. S., & Schumm, J. S. (2006). *Teaching exceptional, diverse, and at-risk students in the general education classroom* (3rd ed.). Upper Saddle River, NJ: Pearson.

Vaughn, S., Fletcher, J. M., Francis, D. J., Denton, C. A., Wanzek, J., Wexler, J, et al. (2008). Response to intervention with older students with reading difficulties. *Learning and Individual Differences, 18,* 338–345.

Vaughn, S., & Linan-Thompson, S. (2004). *Research-based methods of reading instruction: Grades K–3.* Alexandria, VA: Association for Supervision and Curriculum Development.

Vaughn, S., & Roberts, G. (2007). Secondary interventions in reading: Providing additional instruction for students at risk. *Teaching Exceptional Children, 39,* 40–46.

Videen, J., Deno, S. L., & Marston, D. (1982). *Correct word sequences: A valid indicator of writing proficiency in written expression* (Research Rep. No. 84). Minneapolis: Institute for Research on Learning Disabilities.

Welch, M. (1992). The PLEASE strategy: A metacognitive learning strategy for improving the paragraph writing of students with mild learning disabilities. *Learning Disability Quarterly, 15,* 119–128.

Wheelock, W. H., Campbell, C., & Silvaroli, N. J. (2008). *Classroom reading inventory.* Columbus, OH: McGraw Hill.

Wiig, E. H. (2000). Authentic and other assessments of language disabilities: When is fair fair? *Reading and Writing Quarterly, 16,* 179–210.

Wiley, H. I., & Deno, S. L. (2005). Oral reading and maze measures as predictors of success for English learners on a state standards assessment. *Remedial and Special Education, 26,* 207–214.

Wolford, T. L., Heward, W. L., & Alber, S. R. (2001). Teaching middle school students with learning disabilities to recruit peer assistance during cooperative learning group activities. *Learning Disabilities Research and Practice, 16,* 161–173.

Wong, Y. L., Butler, D. L., Ficzere, S. A., & Kuperis, S. (1996). Teaching low achievers and students with learning disabilities to plan, write, and revise opinion essays. *Journal of Learning Disabilities, 29,* 197–212.

Wong, Y. L., Butler, D. L., Ficzere, S. A., & Kuperis, S. (1997). Teaching adolescents with learning disabilities and low achievers to plan, write, and revise compare-and-contrast essays. *Learning Disabilities Research and Practice, 12,* 2–15.

Wood, F. H., & Thompson, S. R. (1993). Assumptions about staff development based on research and best coaching. *Journal of Staff Development, 14,* 52–57.

Woods, M. L., & Moe, A. J. (2003). *Analytical reading inventory.* (7th ed.). Upper Saddle River, NJ: Merrill/Prentice Hall.

Workforce Investment Act. (1998). *Public Law 105-220.* Retrieved December 11, 2009, from http://www.doleta.gov/regs/statutes/wialaw.txt

Wright, J. (2001). *The savvy teacher's guide: Reading interventions that work.* Retrieved December 20, 2009, from http://www.asec.net/Archives/SLD/Reading IntervenMan.pdf

Yopp, H. K. (1992). Developing phonemic awareness in young children. *The Reading Teacher, 45,* 696–703.

Yopp, H. K., & Yopp, R. H. (2000). Supporting phonemic awareness development in the classroom. *The Reading Teacher, 54,* 130–144.

Index